The Art of
Revolver Shooting

THE AUTHOR

The Art of
Revolver Shooting

Walter Winans

LEONAUR

The Art of Revolver Shooting
by Walter Winans

First published under the title
The Art of Revolver Shooting

Leonaur is an imprint of Oakpast Ltd

Copyright in this form © 2013 Oakpast Ltd

ISBN: 978-1-78282-094-9 (hardcover)
ISBN: 978-1-78282-095-6 (softcover)

http://www.leonaur.com

Publisher's Notes

Contents

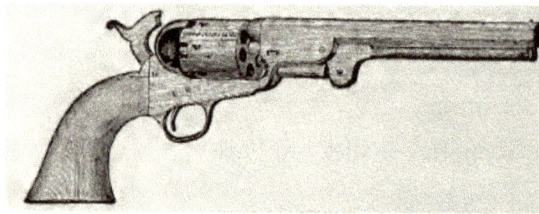

ORIGINAL COLT REVOLVER

Preface

I constantly receive letters from all parts of the world asking my advice on pistol and revolver matters. It seemed, therefore, that there was a want of information on this subject. I tried to supply this information in the first edition of *The Art of Revolver Shooting*, I wrote in 1901, in which I gave further and fuller details than could be given in separate letters to those who have done me the honour of consulting me.

My book was, therefore, of some use to beginners who have no one at hand to show them how to set to work, but since then many improvements have been made in pistols and revolvers, so that the time seemed to have come for me to write a second edition of the book, in which all the information given would be brought well up to date. This I have done, adding a chapter on automatic and duelling pistols, there not having been any previous work published which deals with the latter.

Working a thing out for yourself is always a much longer process than being started in the right way at first; and you may get into a bad way of doing things, which it is hard later to unlearn. Also, you may be working on a line which has already been tried and found wanting, and which therefore renders your labour a mere waste of time.

I do not think that anyone who takes up pistol and revolver shooting—for other than man-killing purposes—will ever regret it. It is not only morally and physically a healthy sport, but it teaches self-reliance, coolness, and the control of one's temper, which last such amusements as croquet and golf, for instance, certainly do not. Pistol shooting is also an accomplishment always useful and sometimes of vital importance. It is thus unlike croquet, cricket, lawn-tennis, golf, and all other games which develop skill only in forms that cannot be of practical use. It may be objected that the games I condemn are useful as exercises for the development of the body; but there are plenty of forms of sports—shooting, hunting, swimming, polo, bicycling, and so on—which give just as good, or better, exercise, yet at the same time teach skill in something useful instead of in mere play fit only for boys.

If men spent in seeking to attain proficiency with the rifle, the pistol, or even the shotgun, a twentieth part of the time they at present devote to playing useless games, they would make their country invincible. Wellington is said to have declared that battles were won on the playgrounds. That may have been the case in times when men shot with "gas-pipes" and needed only to "loose off," the direction of the bullet having little relation to the aim taken. With modern arms of precision, however, the battles of the future will be won in the forest and at the rifle-range.

The difficulty of finding sufficient rifle-ranges in a densely populated country is one that will increase as time goes on, but meanwhile it should be borne in mind that, with gallery ammunition, a five-yards' range in any odd corner or cellar is ample space for pistol practice. It may moreover fairly be claimed that the greater difficulty of pistol shooting makes it a valuable training in the use of the rifle, though the converse by no means holds. The nation that is not a "shooting nation" will "get left" in war time. I hope, however, that as countries become more civilised they will pay greater heed to the idea of arbitration in place of war, the idea which was so nobly inaugurated by His Imperial Majesty the Emperor of Russia (my fatherland), and that by the time the pistol becomes obsolete there will be no need of a weapon to take its place, but that the revolver and war will die out together.

W. W.

Surrenden Park,
Kent, England, 1910.

WORLD'S CHAMPIONSHIP GOLD
MEDAL OLYMPIC GAMES 1908

CHAPTER 3

Evolution of the Revolver

The single-shot pistol, as soon as rifling and the copper cap were invented, quickly attained great accuracy. In fact the modern duelling pistol, the most accurate up to the present time of large calibre pistols, is practically identical with the Joe Manton pistol, though the revolver is still being improved upon. For accuracy it is today ahead of automatic pistols. The revolver is by no means the embodiment of a modern idea; some of the very earliest firearms involved the principle of a revolving cylinder or of revolving barrels, but none was practicable with flint-, wheel-, or match-locks. The introduction of the copper cap enabled Colonel Colt to make the first practical revolving pistol, and "fixed" ammunition made possible the production of breech-loading revolvers.

There have been a few attempts to improve on the revolver by going back to modifications of the old "pepper-box," or many-barrelled pistol, but the mechanical difficulties of making so many barrels shoot "together" do not hold out much hope of success in that direction. Before Colonel Colt took up the problem of designing a practical revolver, many such attempts had been made on wrong lines, and even the purpose of a revolver was misunderstood. Even now this is not clearly grasped by some, for only a few years ago a man gravely assured the public, in letters addressed to various news-papers, that a revolver was of no use because he did not consider that it shot accurately at two hundred yards and upwards! Imagine anyone wanting to shoot at such distances with a revolver! Still, up to four hundred yards it is possible to hit a "second-class" rifle target.

Owing to the shortness necessary to make a revolver a portable arm, the barrel cannot be made to shoot as accurately as a long rifle-barrel will shoot. Also, owing to the sights on a revolver being neces-

ANCIENT FLINT-LOCK PISTOLS

VIEW SHOWING BARRELS HALF REVOLVED

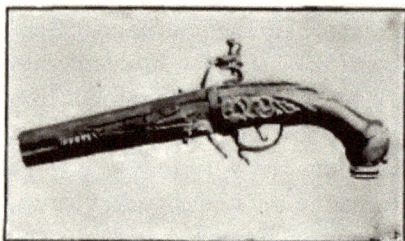

BARRELS IN THE FIRING POSITION
Colonial flint-and-steel revolver.
Age 170 to 200 years.

sarily so close together, at long ranges the accuracy of aim attainable with a rifle cannot be Obtained with a revolver, even supposing that the barrel of the latter could be made to shoot as well as a rifle-barrel. Match rifle-shots have, for this reason, their hind-sights placed at the end of the stock instead of on the breech end of the barrel, in order to have the sights as far apart as possible, while the modern Belgian match pistol, described later, is sighted on a somewhat similar principle. The adjustable butt shown here is intended to enable the revolver to be shot accurately at its extreme limit of range.

Colonel Colt, however, knew better than to think that a revolver should shoot well up to two hundred yards. He understood that there was need for a very small, compact arm, which could be fired very rapidly for self-defence *at close quarters*, still more at "half-arm distance," when a rifle would be useless. The single-shot pistols left a man defenceless after he had fired his one shot, unless he stuck his belt full of pistols like a stage pirate.

At first some curious attempts were made to transform a five-or six-chambered revolver into a ten-or twelve-shot one by *loading each chamber twice over; that is to say by putting one charge in and then another on the top of it.* The front charge was fired first, then the one behind it,—that is, when the two charges did not go off simultaneously and burst the revolver! This naturally was found to be an unpractical and a dangerous system; indeed that any sane man could have thought out such a combination seems almost incredible. I have often found, however, when rummaging among old patents, harebrained devices of this nature. I have also seen a fourteen-shot revolver with two barrels, one below the other, the cylinder having a double set of chambers, the inner set for the lower barrel!!

I have had one or two revolvers made with the "saw-handle" of the old duelling pistols. I have won with them at Bisley and found such stocks very good for deliberate shooting, or rather, when only one shot has to be fired. But it is necessary to use both hands for cocking, as the projection which comes over the fork of the thumb prevents one-handed cocking. It would be suitable for double-action revolvers. Most likely Colt also found this difficulty, and that is the reason for his having invented the typical revolver handle, which, with slight modifications, is used in most revolvers.

A Dutch friend of mine invented a very good handle grip for deliberate shooting. He put a lump of modelling wax on the handle, gripped it hard till it took the impression of his fingers and palm, and

Bow-Pistol

1525

Matchlock

WHEEL-LOCK

FLINT-LOCK

PERCUSSIONLOCK

REVOLVER

then had it cast in metal. It makes a very "hot" grip, but this can be partly overcome by having it hollow, open at the bottom, and pierced with holes.

EXTENSION STOCK AS APPLIED TO .44 SINGLE-ACTION REVOLVER

CHAPTER 4

Selecting a Pistol

Do not buy a cheap revolver or pistol by an unknown maker. Not only is it very dangerous to the shooter to use a weapon of the kind, but nobody can make any shooting with it.

If you do not wish to pay a long price for your pistol, rather buy a second-hand one by a good maker than a new one of inferior pattern. It is of importance, however, to ascertain that the rifling is still perfect, that is to say that it has not suffered deterioration from neglect or wear.

You must first decide for what purpose you want the pistol; a "general utility" weapon is of about as much use as a hunter that is also a harness horse—not much good for either purpose. If you want a hunter, buy an Irish one; if a harness horse, get an American trotter. In the same way, for whatever purpose you want a pistol, buy one, if by any means you can do so, especially for that purpose. Anyhow, it is useless to compete with a short-barrelled pocket revolver, or with an automatic pistol, against duelling pistols, .22 single-shot, or target revolvers.

The former class of revolver is intended only for self-defence at short range, and has no pretensions to accuracy; but a good single-shot pistol can beat almost any revolver. I should have left out the word "almost" had I not seen Ira Paine's Gold Medal score at sixteen metres at Gastinne Renette's which beats any single-shot pistol score that I have as yet come across.

Read the chapter carefully which describes the particular purpose for which you want the pistol, and buy accordingly.

I think that six and a half inches in the barrel, *exclusive* of cylinder, is about the most practical length for a revolver; of course, a longer barrel theoretically gives greater accuracy, especially at long range, owing

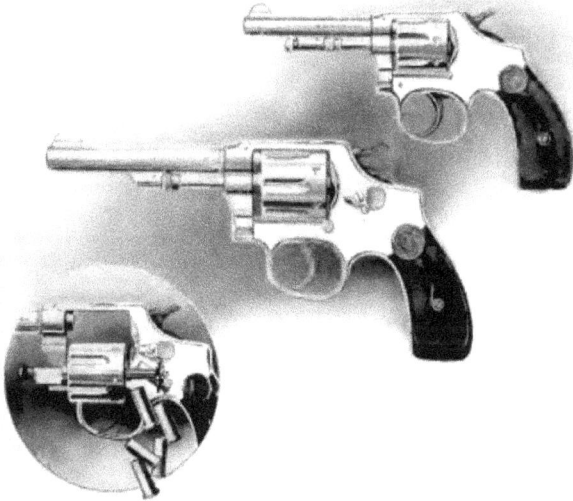

Sᴍɪᴛʜ & Wᴇssᴏɴ Nᴇᴡ Sᴏʟɪᴅ-Fʀᴀᴍᴇ Rᴇᴠᴏʟᴠᴇʀs ғᴏʀ
SMOKELESS POWDER

Sᴇᴄᴛɪᴏɴ ᴏғ ᴄʏʟɪɴᴅᴇʀ, sʜᴏᴡɪɴɢ
HARDENED STEEL SHIMS UNFINISHED

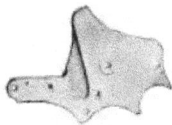

Sɪᴅᴇ ᴘʟᴀᴛᴇ ᴏғ ᴍɪʟɪᴛᴀʀʏ ʀᴇᴠᴏʟᴠᴇʀ,
SHOWING RAISED STEEL BOSSES

to there being more length to burn the powder in, also owing to the sights being set farther apart,—the last-named feature minimises error in aiming. This advantage, however, is more than counterbalanced by its making the revolver heavy at the muzzle, in consequence of which it must balance badly. The duelling pistol has the barrel fluted forward, which allows the barrel to be twelve inches long and yet balance well, and the fourteen-inch size pistol projects backward over the hand and thus balances. The balance ought in every case to be as near the trigger as possible. For a pocket revolver, a short barrel may be an absolute necessity for portability. At Bisley some men use very long barrels, and I believe seven-and-a-half-inch barrels are not unusual in their revolvers; but I prefer six and a quarter inches, exclusive of chamber, and I do not consider—although the Bisley rules allow it—that anything over that length in the barrel is a "Military" revolver or should be permitted to be used in military competitions.

See that the trigger-pull is "sweet," and that it has no "drag." Also, have your trigger-pull not over four and a half pounds. The pull is often left very heavy, so as to be alterable to suit customers, and the shopman may forget to have this altered. If you are not hampered by rules, about three or three and a half pounds is the best trigger-pull for general purposes. Have the thumb-piece of the hammer slightly roughed to prevent slipping. For rapid cocking, a rather long thumb-piece is an advantage, if it is a single-action revolver. But revolvers are now made with such good double action that the latter is preferable except for extreme accuracy.

I disliked a double-action revolver, except for a pocket revolver, as with the older makes one could not do accurate shooting when cocking with the trigger; but the Smith & Wesson double-action .38 Military shoots very well, and with the French regulation revolver, with the former action, I have put the six shots in a two-and-a-quarter-inch space at twenty-five metres in twelve seconds.

For a man whose hands are apt to get moist, roughing the trigger may prevent its slipping. It will, however, also make the finger sore if roughed too sharp; it can be covered with rubber with advantage.

Some pistols have too narrow a trigger, almost like a piece of wire. A wide, spoon-shaped trigger is best, as less likely to cut the ringer, especially with the regulation English heavy trigger-pull.

Get a pistol which, when you grip the stock properly, has the barrel and your arm as nearly in a horizontal line as possible. Many makes of revolvers, and all the automatic pistols so far produced, have the

Engraved .38 Smith & Wesson

Engraved Russian Model, Smith & Wesson

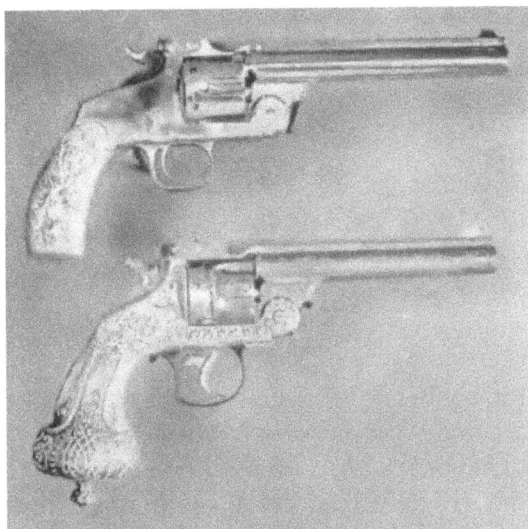

Elaborately carved revolvers
Owned by the Author

stock much below the level of the barrel, and the chambers and barrel are, consequently, far above the hand. This makes shooting more difficult; you are apt to cant the weapon to one side, and the recoil is more severe on your wrist. The French duelling pistol has the handle ideally placed, which makes it much easier to shoot than the average revolver. Most of the .22 calibre single-shot pistols have the trigger too near the hand. Do not get a revolver with a big stock, "specially made for the English market." These big stocks spoil the balance, and are clumsy. A man who holds a revolver properly does not need a big stock, even if he has a big hand.

Writing of revolvers reminds me of an incident that is said to have occurred during the Franco-Prussian war, showing the advantage of a revolver over a sword in battle.

A French cavalry soldier during a *mêlée* with Prussian cavalry kept several of the latter's troopers at bay by pointing his revolver at them in turn, although the revolver was empty, the cartridges it contained having all been discharged. Then, thinking he would be safer with a sword than with an empty revolver, he suddenly threw away the latter and drew his sword, with the result that he was at once cut down by the nearest Prussian.

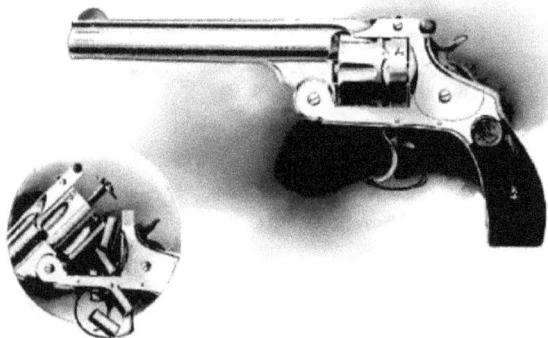

SMITH & WESSON .44 DOUBLE-ACTION REVOLVER

Shown opposite are illustrations of the four principal makes of revolvers: Smith & Wesson ("Winans' Model"), "Bisley" Colt, "Target" Webley, and Smith & Wesson double-action Military.

I won my championships the first few years with a .45 double-action cavalry Colt, using Eley's .45 black powder ammunition. Since then I have shot with the Smith & Wesson revolvers, either the . 44 calibre Russian Model, the .45 Winans' Model, the .32 and .38 cali-

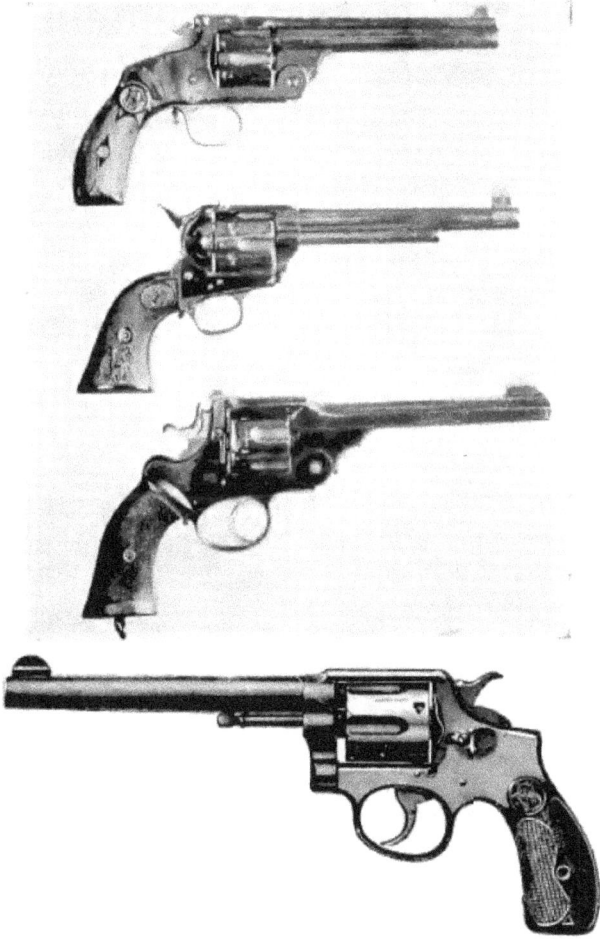

THE FOUR PRINCIPAL REVOLVERS: SMITH & WESSON (" WINANS MODEL"), "BISLEY" COLT, "TARGET" WEBLEY, AND SMITH & WESSON MILITARY.

bre in Russian Model frame, the .38 Military double-action Smith & Wesson, and the Dutch and the French army-revolvers. The first I use with gallery ammunition, U. M. C. cartridges, French revolver powder, as my sixteen-metres, twenty-five-metres, and twenty-yards "Any" or target revolver; the same revolver with full charge as " Military" for fifty yards; the Winans' Model sometimes both as "Military" and "Any" alternative revolver at twenty or fifty yards, the .32 being my fifty-yards "Any" revolver; the .38 Military Smith & Wesson for rapid firing in the French Competitions at twenty-five metres, and the Dutch for competing at thirty metres in that country.

One of the reasons why the Smith & Wesson revolver is so accurate is because so much care is taken by the makers to have cylinder and barrel in perfect alignment; and it is not too much to say that I have never shot any revolver of any other make which I can so safely trust not to give me a wild shot.

To secure this result, the stop and stop-notch, which arrest the momentum of the cylinder and hold it in position during discharge, play the most important part. In all cheap revolvers the notches are made in the soft steel of the cylinder, and in consequence these notches soon wear, putting the alignment out, which prevents accuracy. When the notch gets too much worn, this makes firing the revolver even a positive danger. In the Smith & Wesson revolver this is obviated by a piece of hard steel being fitted into the side of the notch which comes in contact with the stop when the motion of the cylinder is checked. This is a special patent of the firm.

This make of revolver also has steel bosses, or collars fitted into the frame, to keep the hammer, trigger, etc., from coming in contact with the sides of the frame. Lately this firm have an additional arrangement for securing perfect concentric joining of the bore of the chamber and barrel.

I merely designed the Winans' Model revolver to suit former Bisley rules as to "Military" revolvers, and would have used the Russian Model in preference, had the rules permitted; but the Russian and United States army revolvers were not considered "Military" revolvers by those rules.

Ornamentation in a revolver is a matter of taste. Personally, I prefer my "tools" to be as plain as possible, without any engraving. All projecting screw-heads, etc., should be filed down flat to prevent their chafing the hand; the trigger and thumb-piece of the hammer may also be cross-filed to prevent slipping, but not filed "sharp" enough

SMITH & WESSON MILITARY REVOLVERS

to make one's thumb or finger sore; and I prefer a chequered rubber stock.

I have my revolvers gold-, silver-, or copper-plated all over, not for show, but to prevent a man's using one of mine and saying, "So sorry—thought it was mine, don't you know!" if in a competition I inadvertently leave a revolver of mine on the firing ledge.

By having the colour of the plating varied, you know at a glance if you have the right revolver for the particular work in hand: your "gold" for twenty yards; "copper" for rapid firing; "silver" for fifty yards, and so on.

For rough work, and in strong sunlight, a revolver is best blued. I temporarily paint the rib, etc., with "sight black," when competing on sunny days. The pearl stocks, though looking slippery, really give one a very good hold; when one's hand gets warm they stick to the skin as if they were resined. Ira Paine always used pearl stocks.

The most ornamental revolver I have ever seen is the one shown in the lower illustration on page 19, which was presented to me. It is in silver and carved ivory, decorated by Tiffany, and was the main attraction in the Revolver Section of the Chicago Exhibition. It is, I believe, the most costly revolver that has yet been made. The other has a silver handle bearing deer-heads modelled by myself, the screw-heads forming the eyes of the deer.

I also have a very artistic pair of revolver "stock-plates." These I had made in ivory and sent to Japan to be inlaid with gold and coloured stones. I left the design to the native artist, and he put a Japanese hawk-ing scene on one, and on the other a picture of duck-shooting with bow and arrow.

Of single-shot pistols by far the best, though also the most expensive, is the Gastinne-Renette, a .44 calibre muzzle-loading duelling pistol, shooting a round ball and French smokeless powder. The same makers' .22 calibre single-shot pistol, the Stevens, and Leeson .22 are also very good. They are described in later chapters.

Of course, the revolver in its present form will have to give place to something better. I rather think the multi-shot pistol of the future will be on the revolver principle, but with a means of making a tight joint, at the moment of firing, between the cylinder and the barrel; or that the cartridge will be automatically pushed out of the cylinder into the barrel and fired from there; also that the cartridges, containing some condensed powder, will be much shorter, so that the cylinder can also be shortened. Likewise the cocking and the cylinder-revolving will be done automatically by the recoil.

In prices revolvers vary greatly. The Smith & Wesson costs about £5. The Webley solid frame averages £3 in blue, and £3.ios. in nickel. The "Ex-tractor," Mark III., .38, by the same makers, comes to £4. 1 6s. Morris Tubes for revolvers (not less than .320) costs from £1. 5s. 6d. to £1. 10s. 6d. The Morris Tube Co.'s Trajectory Target (steel, for fifty yards) costs £3. 3s., and their Safety Mantlet (7 feet x 3 x 3) costs £10, and Butt (7 feet x 3) £2. 10s.

CHAPTER 5

Ammunition

My aim throughout this work is to make the book as complete as possible on the subject of pistols,—single-shot pistols, revolvers, and automatic repeating pistols.

It was my original intention to give illustrations and minute descriptions of all modern pistols and ammunition, taking both black and smokeless powders; but I found that this would tend to make the chapters on pistols and ammunition resemble gunmakers' catalogues. Therefore I illustrate only typical instances, and those pistols and ammunition with which I have won prizes and that, having used constantly, I know to be good.

Revolver ammunition is usually made in the following calibres: .32, .38, .41, .44, .45, .455, and .457. Most of these can be had loaded with various smokeless powders, as King's semi-smokeless, Riflite, Cordite, Walsrode, French Revolver, etc.

The Union Metallic Cartridge Company, U. S. A., have supplied me with great quantities of .44 "gallery ammunition," loaded with both round and semi-round bullets. These have a small charge of black powder, and I preferred this ammunition out of a Smith & Wesson Russian Model revolver for self-defence, as well as for competitions up to twenty-five yards, and I found it the most accurate of any for exhibition shooting. I believe most professional stage-shooters use it for revolvers and the .22 shot for single-shot Stevens pistols. I now have found an even better load, which is the French smokeless powder. This does not foul, or lead, and one can shoot hundreds of shots without cleaning. I only use that now in U. M. C. shells for the .44 Smith & Wesson and the .38 Army Model Smith & Wesson revolvers.

I suppose the various English makers of ammunition could supply "gallery" charges in any of their various calibre cartridges, but I know

.32-.44 is a special target cartridge, containing 11 grs. of powder and 83 grs. of lead. Bullet seated even with mouth of shell. Penetration, 5 ⅞-in. pine boards. Gallery charge, 6 grs. of powder and 50 gr. round ball loaded in same shell.

.38-.44 is also a special target cartridge, containing 20 grs. of powder and 146 of lead, either self-lubricating or grooved bullet. Bullet is seated even with mouth of shell. Penetration, 6 ⅞-in. pine boards. Gallery charge, 6 grs. of powder and 70 gr. round ball loaded in same shell.

.38 Winchester rifle cartridge, containing 40 grs. of powder and 180 grs. of lead. Penetration, 7 ⅞-in. pine boards.

.44 Russian Model is a cartridge for long-range target work. It contains 23 grs. of powder and 256 grs. of lead. Bullets are either self-lubricating or the regular grooved. Penetration, 7½ ⅞-in. pine boards. Gallery charge, 7 grs. of powder and 110 gr. round ball loaded in same shell.

.44 Winchester is the regular model 73 Winchester rifle cartridge, and contains 40 grs. of powder and 217 grains of lead. Penetration, 6½ ⅞-in. pine boards.

.450 cartridge contains 13 grs. of powder and 226 grs. of lead. English or American cartridges can be used.

Powder, 5 gr.; bullet, 40 gr.; exact cal.. 0.223

Powder, 3 gr.; bullet, 30 gr.; exact cal. 0.223.

Powder, 10 gr.; bullet, 88 gr.; exact cal., 0.313.

Powder, 13 gr.; bullet, 100 gr.; exact cal., 0.313.

Powder, 13 gr.; bullet, 100 gr.; exact cal., 0.313.

of none and should not advise the beginner to try loading this sort of ammunition in English cartridge-cases for himself. The dome of the cap is generally higher than in American cartridges if, therefore, a very small quantity of powder be put in the case and the bullet pressed down, the bullet will come down on the dome, stop up the flash hole, and cause a misfire. The way to obviate this is to take a wad of suitable calibre, make a hole in the centre, and push the wad down to the bottom of the cartridge before putting in the powder, so as to fill up the base of the cartridge and let the bullet "seat" on the powder, higher than the dome. Makers can do this properly, but an amateur may put the wad in too loosely, and a grain or so of powder may get under the wad. The result would be that, on the shot being fired, the wad would be driven half-way up the barrel, and might at the next shot cause an accident.

Be sure to use only low-pressure powder, if you use smokeless, as high-pressure powders are dangerous in a revolver.

Many people do not understand this difference in and powder pressure, and injure their revolvers by experimenting with what become practically "blasting instead of propelling charges. For the twenty-yards "Military" competitions at Bisley, in which one is not allowed to use less than thirteen grains of black powder (or its equivalent in muzzle velocity of smokeless), and 216 ½ grs. of lead in the bullet, or less than .45 calibre, I have used Eley's .45 black powder cartridges and the Union Metallic Cartridge Company's similar ammunition in most of my competitions. I think the Union Metallic Company's gives rather less recoil and fewer " unaccountable" than the English equivalent; I suppose it has a slower-burning powder. That is why, of late years, I have confined myself to the use of it. They also load these cartridges with King's semi-smokeless powder, which I have used, and with which I have made my "bests-on-record" in the rapid-firing competitions at twenty yards.

At twenty-five metres my record score made in Paris, April 6th 1909, was with French smokeless powder in U. M. C. shells, and at thirty metres with Dutch smokeless, and for the fifty-yards competitions I have used these two makes of .45 calibre ammunition (with black powder); but my "best-on-record" scores at this distance were made with the Union Metallic Cartridge Company's .44 calibre and .32 calibre cartridges, loaded respectively with twenty-three and twenty-six grains of black powder, with the Smith & Wesson "Self-lubricating bullet."

The .38 Smith & Wesson special
contains 21½ grains of black powder and 158-grain solid base
bullet. Penetration, eight and
one-half ⅞-inch pine boards. This
is a very powerful charge and extremely accurate. Gallery charge
6 grains of powder and 70-grain
round ball loaded in same shell.

The regular .38 United
States service cartridge (listed
as .38 long Colt) is used in
the same revolver and is very
accurate, but not so powerful
as the special. It contains
18 grains of black powder
and 150-grain hollow base
bullet. Penetration, six and
one-half ⅞-inch pine boards.

The .32 Winchester is the regular Winchester repeating-rifle
cartridge. It is very accurate and
powerful and gives good results
up to 200 yards. It contains 20
grains of black powder and 115-
grain bullet. Penetration, six and
one-half ⅞-inch pine boards.

I have also done very good shooting with the ordinary Union Metallic Cartridge Company's .44 Russian Model ammunition, twenty-three grains of black powder, and an ordinary bullet.

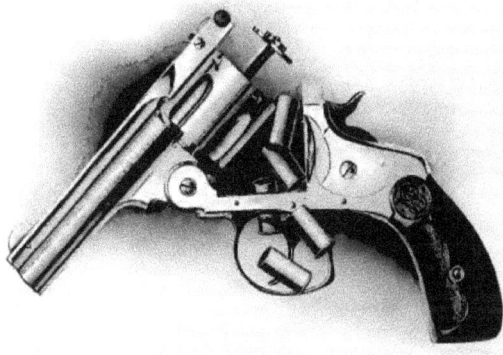

Automatic shell extractor as applied to all jointed frame models of the Smith & Wesson Revolvers

I find that in competing at fifty yards one *must*, if physically strong enough to stand it, shoot a big charge in the larger calibre revolvers to get the greatest accuracy; with a .22 calibre single-shot pistol this is not necessary. The charge of twenty-three grains of black powder has a very heavy recoil, heavier than the English army .457 ammunition. I do not think that any other competitor at Bisley uses such a heavy load. The .32 with eleven grains powder charge has not an unpleasant recoil. It is not nearly as heavy in the .32 Smith & Wesson Russian Model (.44 "frame," .32 calibre) as the .45 with thirteen grains powder in a .45 calibre, and is very accurate at fifty yards; but by the Bisley rules it cannot be used in "Military Revolver" competitions, though it is allowed in Continental military competitions. The solid frame Smith & Wesson revolvers with smokeless powder are an improvement on their old black powder "break-down" models.

Never use any ammunition different from that recommended by the makers of the particular revolver you are using, without consulting them. I have had several narrow escapes (in one case having a bullet stop half-way in the barrel) when experimenting with various powders suitable for rifles but not for revolvers.

The new model Smith & Wesson cartridge with "Self-lubricating bullet" (see diagram) is specially designed to prevent fouling and so do away with the necessity of constantly cleaning a revolver whilst shoot-

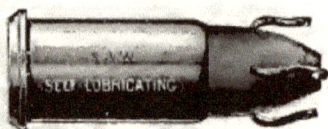

COMPLETE SELF-LUBRICATING
CARTRIDGE

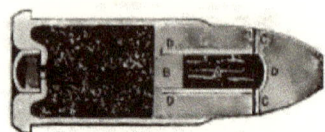

CUT SHOWING DETAILS OF
CONSTRUCTION

A, Lubricant; B, Plunger; C, Ducts;
D, Metal Lining

EXPLANATION.—At the moment of explosion, the lead plunger (B), being driven forward, forces the lubricant contained in the cavity (A) out through the ducts (C) in front of the bullet, and at a point most effective.

The ducts being completely closed by the plunger, all escape of gas and loss of force is consequently prevented.

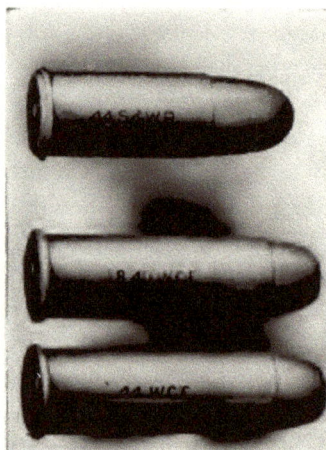

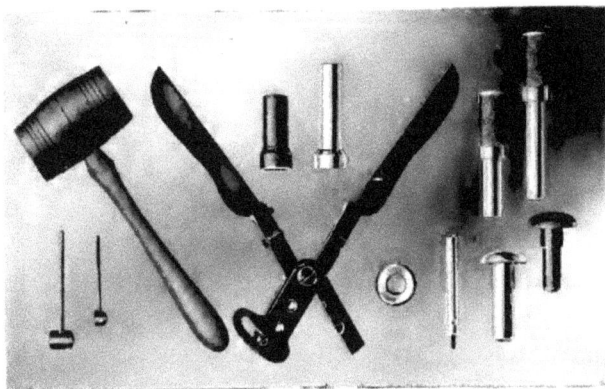

RELOADING TOOLS

ing black powder. The bullet is self-lubricating, instead of carrying its lubricant in canilures. In this bullet a better lubricant is used (or perhaps it lubricates better) than that which can be held in canilures; and it is forced by the explosion into the grooves of the barrel *in front of*, instead of behind, the bullet. This is, of course, the more correct principle, for the bullet, being smooth without any canilure, gets an easier bearing on the rifling. It is made in regular .32, .38, and .44 calibres, also in .32 long, and special .38. Bullets are also sold separately. I made my record at Bisley at fifty yards with this bullet and twenty-three grains black powder.

Messrs. Smith & Wesson do not guarantee their "break-down" action revolvers. They guarantee their new solid-frame revolvers when used with smokeless powder (smokeless powder cartridges are now made for the .44 Russian Model revolver) and I would warn my readers to be very careful when trying experiments with such powders in revolvers; to use only those recommended by the makers of the revolver used; and not to try loading them themselves. Such powders also need special primers and pressures. The French smokeless powder I consider the best of all for gallery ammunition, and you can shoot hundreds of shots without cleaning. Moreover in a double-action it does not jam the revolver as powders do which foul more.

The average cost of revolver ammunition is 2s. 6d. for fifty cartridges. Kynoch's solid-drawn brass cartridges (for Smith & Wesson and Webley revolvers) run to about £2. 15s. a thousand for .44; £2. 7s. 6d for .38; and £1. 1 6s. 8d. for .32.

CHAPTER 6

Cleaning and Care of Weapons

Always clean your pistol the moment you have finished shooting. If you leave it over till the next day you may as well throw it away as expect to win prizes with it.

The larger the calibre, the easier it is to clean and the less chance is there of spoiling the rifling by jamming the rod in it. I prefer wooden rods as less apt to spoil the rifling, but the very narrow calibres require a metal rod (soft metal for preference), as the wood would have to be too thin, and would be liable to break in the bore.

Clean from the breech, not from the muzzle end, except of course the muzzle-loading duelling pistol; the last fraction of an inch at the muzzle is where the rifling, if damaged, spoils the shooting most. For the same reason it is as well to have the rifling "reamed off" at the mouth of the muzzle so that the edge of it is protected. If you use nitro-powders, examine the interior of your barrel at frequent intervals after cleaning, to see if there is any damage going on.

Use the cleaning fluids recommended for the particular powder you are using, as what may be good for one powder is of no use for another. I use Hillias' cleaning fluid, finishing up with Marlin gun-grease, but there are special mixtures for cleaning after using cordite. Where nickel-covered bullets are used a special chemical dissolves the nickel left in the barrel.

The great thing is to clean thoroughly. I use cotton-wool of the best quality rather than tow, and I do not use boiling water unless in very exceptional cases, for fear of overlooking a spot in drying, and getting rust in consequence. If necessary to use water to remove fouling, let it be as hot as possible.

Do not try to oil the lock, or put it right; send it occasionally to the maker to be seen to. It is also well to have a cleaning kit with wooden, not metal (except for calibres of .32 or less) cleaning rods, cotton-wool, cleaning fluids, screw-drivers, etc., all in proper compartments, *and put back* when used. See that the cotton-wool is absolutely dry and clean before using it. Throw away such pieces as are used. "Selvit" cut to proper size like shotgun wads is a good finish to push through the barrel. Do not use too big a piece on your rod, such as would get the latter jammed in the barrel, as you may ruin the shooting qualities of the barrel by using force to remove it. Have the cleaning rods long enough or you may bark your knuckles.

I also do not like the cardboard cases in which American pistols are usually packed, for permanent use; they are not strong enough and are apt to injure the sights, especially fine sights. A holster, again, is not the thing in which to keep a revolver habitually, as the sights get knocked about; also if the holster is used out-of-doors it gets damp inside and rusts the weapon. Great care should always be taken to see that the holster is absolutely dry in-side before placing a revolver therein. To dry the inside of a holster, make some oats very hot in a saucepan, and fill the holster with them, emptying them out when cold. Some American holsters are made of india-rubber, to prevent perspiration from the body rusting the revolver, but such are very liable to retain dampness inside. The holster which I prefer (for wearing, and *not* as a pistol-case) is a cowboy holster, without any button to the flap. If you fasten the flap, you cannot get the pistol out in a hurry. A lining of rabbit fur is useful to keep out sand or dust.

My pistol-cases are good, strong, and solid, made of leather, with brass corners like gun-cases. Each case holds four, placed either side by side, each pistol in its own compartment, or, with a tray, two in the tray and two below. If you have only two, they can be put in a case without this upper tray, or the tray can be used for cartridges. Under all circumstances use a good lock,—not the sort that any key fits,—keep the case locked, and wear the key on your watch-chain so that you may be sure nobody will be able to get at it. Keep the case in a dry place, and look at the pistols occasionally, when they are not in constant use, to see that they are not rusting.

Keep your cartridges, if not in the same case as the revolvers, locked in a good leather case. This may be fitted with compartments for various calibres and loads. The word "loaded" may with advantage be inscribed inside the lid of the pistol-cases. People then feel less encouragement to meddle with the contents.

CHAPTER 7

Sights

Sights are made in many forms. Some suit one man best; others another. You cannot decide which suits your individual case without trying each sort for yourself.

When you find one form which suits you, it is a pity to risk spoiling your shooting by changing to others; a beginner should never do so, or he will get into an uncertain way of taking his sights, instead of using always the same, the only way to make reliable, consistent shooting. Of course, all your sights may be of no use if you are going to shoot in a competition, owing to the authorities making some new rule as to "fit for rough usage." In such a case it will be necessary for you to shoot with whatever sights are allowed by the rules.

My patent sight has, so far, complied with every rule, and it can be used even for hammering nails and yet not surfer damage.

The main point is to have a front sight that is at once easily seen, and of which you see each time the *same amount*, and not more at one time than at another. Unless this is the case you cannot keep your elevation.

Also the "U" in the back sight should have bevelled edges, in order to give a sharp edge; otherwise it looks "woolly."

Again, if you are not able to see daylight each side of the front sight when it is in the "U," you cannot be sure that you are not covering, on one side or the other, part of the front sight. Consequently you cannot tell whether your aim is or is not in horizontal axis with your barrel.

The reason I prefer a "U"-to a "V"-shaped notch in the hind sight is because in the "V" you do not see this daylight so well.

The greater distance between the pistol hind-sight and the eye enables a man with normal power of vision to shoot a pistol without the aid of spectacles up to a more advanced age than is the case

Side view   End view

ELEVATING REAR-SIGHT

Side view   End view

"PAINE" FRONT SIGHT

Side view   End view

FRONT SIGHT

Side view   End view

ELEVATING REAR-SIGHT

Front   Rear

LYMAN SIGHTS

End view of rear   Side view of rear   Side view of front
target sight   target sight

TARGET SIGHTS

with rifle shooting. A healthy eye loses only with age its elasticity or its capacity to adjust the focus to near objects. A rifle hind-sight is of course very near the eye by comparison with the distance of a pistol hind-sight when the arm is at full stretch.

The same principle is involved when an elderly man has to hold a newspaper a long way from his eyes if he wants to read without glasses. I know several men who have come to need glasses for reading, who yet do not need them for pistol shooting.

As soon as you can shoot well enough to know whether bad shots arc the fault of the sighting of the pistol, or of your own holding, you can sight the pistol properly for yourself; and in this way you can do the sighting much more accurately, and with greater nicety, than by taking the weapon to a. gunmaker and saying: "Alter the sights to shoot three inches higher, and two inches to the left at twenty yards, open the 'U' a little," and so on. In-stead, have front and hind sights made of horn, (put in temporarily A without any "U" in the hind sight, and set both hind and front sights a little higher than you think necessary. Then go to the range with your pistol, and take with you files of various sizes, including some that arc round. Make a slight "U" in the *measured* centre of the top edge of the back sight. Shoot a few-shots at the range you want to sight for—taking care that you do not shoot right over the top of the butt, owing to being sighted too high—and then keep working with the files, first at one sight, then at the other, until you get both approximately right.

Do not cut the "U" down too close to the barrel, for if you do it will give you a "blurry" aim, especially when the barrel gets hot. If you find you shoot too high owing to the "U" not being cut down, rather than file the "U" unduly low take out the front sight and put in a higher one. The French duelling pistol has very low sights, and the front one is a stalkless bead, like the sight of a shot-gun, according to French rules these must not be altered or painted. For rapid firing this sort of sighting is very good *till* the barrel gets hot.

When filing, remember the following points:

First, filing the bottom of the "U" makes you shoot *lower*.

Secondly, filing the top of the front sight makes you shoot *higher*.

Thirdly, filing the side of the "U" or the front sight makes you shoot *towards* the side you have filed.

Therefore by filing only a very little at a time where filing is need-ed you can gradually get your sighting perfect. I repeat, be sure to file only a very little at a time, or you will overdo it. As in sculpture, you can easily remove, but you cannot replace. If you do remove too much anywhere you may be able to counteract the fault by filing so as to alter the direction of the aim. For instance, you have been shooting too much to the right. This you can correct by filing the left of the front sight, or the left of the "U,"—whichever makes the more symmetrical job,—but if, in doing so, you make the front sight too small or too narrow, or the "U" too wide, the only thing left to be done is to put in a new front or hind sight as the case may be, and then begin shooting and filing again.

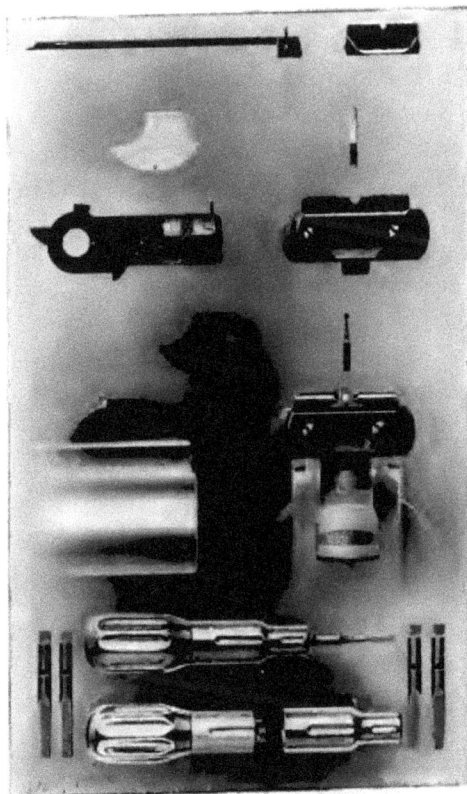

SPECIAL TARGET SIGHTS

When you have got the sighting perfect, work carefully with your file (taking great care not to spoil the edge of the "U" nearest to the eye when aiming), and give a chamfered or bevelled edge to the far side of the "U," so that it has a knife-edge. This is to make the "U" look clear and yet allow the back sight to be strong. On this principle you can let the hind sight be strong, and over a quarter of an inch thick, and yet have a nice, clear "U." Do not have the "U" deeper than a semicircle. If the "U" is too deep it hampers your view of the object aimed at. In fact it really should be a semicircle and not a "U" at all. You can also file all round the front sight, giving it a taper towards the muzzle, but keeping unaltered the silhouette that you see when aiming, so that the outline shall stand out clear to the eye.

A gunmaker's vise, padded in order that it may not injure the weapon held in it, is a useful thing, as it of course leaves the operator's two hands free to use the files; also it proves convenient to hold the pistols in when they are being cleaned.

I cannot tell you how much you may undercut the front sight, assuming you intend to use it on a revolver at Bisley, as the rules alter so from year to year. I have an undercut bead-sight which in some years was allowed at Bisley as a "Military Revolver," and in other years was not. If you are in any doubt as to your weapon's being allowed, the best plan is to send it to the Council of the National Rifle Association for their approval in plenty of time before the Bisley meeting, so that you can alter it if it be not passed.

When you have finished, and have had a final shoot in order to make sure that this finishing has not spoilt your elevation, etc., send your pistol to the maker and ask him to make your sights precisely like your model ones, and to fix them permanently on the revolver— *without screws if for Bisley use,* so as to comply with the rules. If when you get the pistol with, these new sights the work has been properly done, very little more filing will set everything to rights.

Should you not be shooting at Bisley, or at any of those clubs which shoot under Bisley rules, you can, of course, get a pistol with Smith & Wesson's "Ira Paine" adjustable sights. Carry a miniature folding gilt screw-driver and sight-case on your watch chain, as I do, and you will then be able to shoot in any light, at any range, or in any style of shooting, by merely giving a slight turn to the adjusting screws to alter your elevation or direction; or if a sight breaks, or you want one of a different size or shape, you will be able to produce one from your little case of sights.

EXTRACTS FROM SPECIFICATION OF WALTER WINANS'
REVOLVER FRONT-SIGHT

Great difficulty has hitherto been experienced in seeing the same amount of front sight each time aim is taken, unless the base of the sight is sufficiently undercut to form a 'bead sight';

such undercutting being, however, detrimental, as it weakens the 'sight' and renders it very liable to injury, and is not permissible in Bisley revolver competitions. The object of my invention is, therefore, to overcome this difficulty, and to this end I make the 'sight' of metal, horn, wood, or other hard substance, with a strong, wide base, preferably of the 'barleycorn' or triangular section.

The face of the upper part of the 'sight' facing the marks-man (as much of it as it is desirable to see in aiming) is made vertical, or inclined slightly towards the marksman, so as to cause it to appear black, as it is in shadow. The visible part of the sight below the face inclines forward from the marksman, and downward, so as to reflect the light and enable the face of the sight to be at once distinguished by its difference of shade from the lower part. It may be polished or plated to assist in reflecting the light, while, as a contrast, the vertical face is cross-filed, or 'roughed,' or may be hollowed out, so as to be in shadow, and give it a 'dead' black appearance.

In the accompanying drawing overleaf I have shown what I consider the best means of carrying this out. Fig. I is a side view, of a portion of a revolver barrel fitted with my improved 'front-sight.'

Fig. 2 and Fig. 3 are sections of the barrel at A B, showing two forms which the sight may assume in section, one having straight sides, the other concave. I show in Figs. 4 and 4*, on a larger scale, for the sake of clearness, a side and plan view of the sight shown in Fig. 1, and in Fig. 5 a modification of this shape. Figs. 6 and 7 are end views, showing two sectional forms of the sight, and corresponding in size with Figs. 4 and 5. In Figs. 1 and 4 it will be seen that a is the vertical face of the sight, which is designed to present a dark appearance to the marksman; and b is the polished, inclined surface, which takes a rounded form. In the modification, Fig. 5, the face a is slightly inclined towards the marksman, and the bright or polished surface b takes the form of a flat incline.

FIG.1   Fig.2   Fig.3

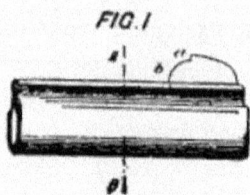

FIG.4.   FIG.5   FIG.8.   FIG.7

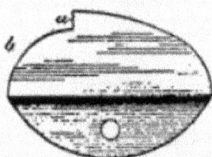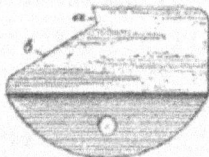

 FIG.4.²

WINANS' REVOLVER FRONT-SIGHTS

CHAPTER 8

Learning to Use the Pistol

It is assumed that you have procured an accurate pistol, properly sighted.

First, open it, or, if it is a muzzle-loader, put in the loading rod and note if it goes in to the chamber, to make sure that it is unloaded. Always do this before handling a pistol.

Take a bottle of sight-black, and paint both sights over with the liquid. I have seen men try to compete, even at Bisley, with their sights in a shiny state, which made it impossible for them to make good shooting on a white target with a black "bull." On the Continent the painting of sights is not allowed in competitions, and very rightly so in my opinion.

For game shooting, or for military purposes, of course a "dead" white (ivory for choice) tip to the front sight is preferable, or my patent military front-sight which answers the purposes both of a light on dark, or dark on light, sight. For the French duelling pistol the front sight must be silver, by the regulations, *not* black.

With a pistol the first thing to consider is safety. It is, owing to its shortness, one of the most dangerous of firearms to handle. Even an expert must exercise great care, whilst in the hands of a beginner or of a careless person it may become fearfully dangerous. I have when teaching men how to shoot had many very narrow escapes from being shot. Indeed in some instances it was not safe even to be behind them, for they would turn round with the pistol at full-cock, and pointing at one, and then perhaps ingenuously remark, "I can't understand why the thing won't go off; look, I am pulling the trigger as hard as I can" (!) Then, a safe background is indispensable. Some people think that if the target is fastened to the trunk of a tree all must be well, since—so they argue—the bullet cannot go through the tree. This may be so if

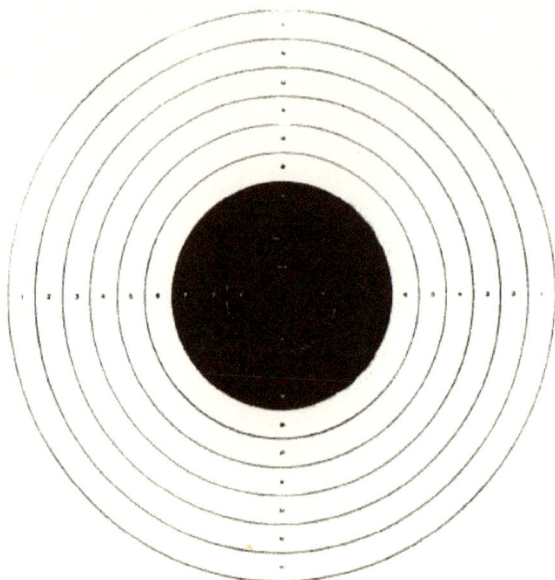

OLYMPIC REGULATION 50 METRES PISTOL TARGET

the tree be hit, but the bullet will, very likely, go past the tree when the beginner fires, or—and this is just as dangerous—it may graze the tree and then go off at a tangent. Also, in shooting with round bullets, and with light gallery ammunition, the bullets may rebound from a hard tree and strike the shooter or someone near him. This I have seen actually happen.

I also remember, many years ago, a servant being told to take an old Colt house-protection muzzle-loader out into the garden, and to empty the chambers there. They had been loaded many years, and the weapon needed reloading to avoid a possible misfire. He fired only one shot, then came back to us limping badly. Asked why he had not fired the rest, he replied that he had "no use" for another shot. It seemed that he had fired at a brick wall, distant only a few feet from him, with the result that the bullet had come back and hit him in the knee.

A good background is a high, sandy bank, a thick pile of fagots, or, if not closer than fifty yards, a high brick or stone wall. The target may be placed fifteen or so yards out from the wall in order to prevent any possible danger through a bullet's coming back on the shooter, who will in any case then be far enough away from the wall for safety. If a lot of shooting be done, and many shots hit the wall at the same spot,

42

a hole may gradually be made in it. This happened in the first year that I shot at Wimbledon, when the butt consisted of old "sleepers." Iron butts are expensive, especially with the large surface required by beginners at twenty yards, for a beginner cannot, in my opinion, shoot with safety at a background less than twelve feet high and about ten feet wide. Even then there should not be anyone within a distance of half a mile beyond it, for a novice may let off his pistol by accident. Shooting out to sea is safe, if a good lookout be kept for boats. The glare from the water, however, is not conducive to accurate marksmanship. A sand- or a chalk-pit is a good place to shoot in; also a high chalk cliff makes a good, safe background. It is of course dangerous to shoot anywhere where people may cross unexpectedly.

A pistol should never under any circumstances be pointed in any direction where it would matter if it went off by accident. This rule should be observed even with an empty pistol, because so many "I-did-not-know-it-was-loaded" accidents have already occurred. Any child seen to point a firearm, even a toy one, at anybody should immediately be given a severe whipping.

The butt which for years I have used for disappearing and stationary targets is an old-fashioned third-class iron rifle target, six feet by four, with a sheet of thick lead one foot square hung in the middle. It is the latter that is struck; the rest of the butt is there merely in case a pistol might be let off unintentionally, say owing to the hammer slipping, or some such cause. The bullets, burying themselves in the lead, do not splash, and the lead falls off in clusters and can be remelted. A beginner, however, would not be able to keep all his shots on the lead alone, so that a butt of this kind is suitable only for a man to use who may be depended upon implicitly, even in rapid firing, to place every bullet on the lead plate, or, in the event of the pistol's being fired unintentionally on the iron butt.

In order to make pistol-and rifle-ranges safe, in 1895 I took out a patent for a safety butt, of which I give a diagram. The following is a description of it:—

In order to diminish the number of ricochets from bullets striking the earth short of the target butts, it is usual to build, at intervals across the range, walls of turf, so that a bullet dropping short of the target will bury itself therein. If, however, a bullet grazes the lop of one of these walls, it will ricochet as badly as ever, particularly if the turf wall or bank is faced with timber, as

THE AUTHOR'S SHOOTING POSITION

is sometimes the case.

To render the turf walls more efficacious than heretofore, I furnish them at their top with a structure from which the bullets will not glance so as to be diverted from their course and caused to assume a dangerous direction.

I apply to the summit of the turf walls or banks a line of planking, the front of which, towards the firing-point, is perpendicular, while the back is chamfered off to a knife-edge at the top. The inclined back of this planking is covered with a layer of felt, india-rubber, or similar soft material, the edge of which projects above the knife-edge of the planking, in a slightly forward direction, towards the firing-point.

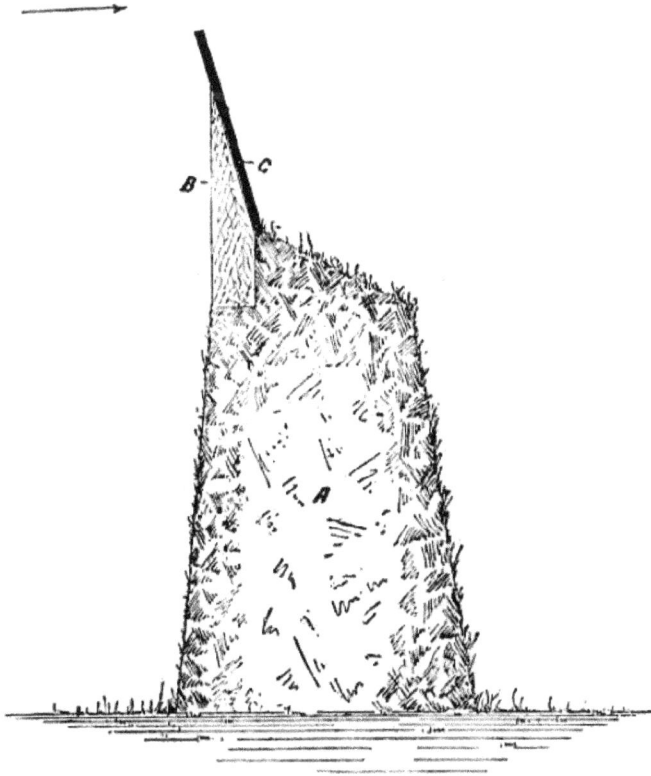

PATENT SAFETY BUTT

In the accompanying drawing I have shown, in end view, a turf wall furnished, in accordance with my invention, with the non-deflecting planking and fell. *A* is the wall or bank of earth covered with turf, which will slop all bullets fired in the direction of the arrow which fairly strike it. *B* is a, wooden rail or plank mounted on the summit of the hank-and having a perpendicular face toward the shooters, and an inclined or chamfered back as shown. *C* is the strip of felt, india-rubber, or other flexible material, attached to the back of the planking *B*, and projecting slightly above the top edge of the said planking in a forward direction. In practice, a bullet grazing the top of the turf wall would be prevented by the planking from glancing away in a danger-ous direction, although the said planking would not stop its course in the direction of the target. In the same way if a bullet touches the topmost edge of the planking, the felt or india-rubber will prevent an upward ricochet; while the bullet, if merely touching the felt or other soft material only, will not be appreciably diverted from its course.

Having got a butt, the learner should take a firm, narrow wooden table and place it some ten yards from the target. This target is prefer-ably a "Bisley fifty-yards target," four-inch bull's-eye. The Bisley card-board targets are cheap, and, by pasting white patches on the white, and black on the bull's-eye bullet-holes, one target can be used for a long time. I refer to the fifty-yards target because this four-inch bull's-eye is very easy to hit at ten yards' range. The Bisley revolver "bull's-eyes" count, at all ranges, seven points; the concentric rings counting one point less, each, till the outermost one, which counts two points. The highest possible score, therefore, for the six shots is forty-two, or six times seven. It is best to shoot at this very big bull at ten yards, as making bull's-eyes encourages the beginner. As he becomes more proficient the two-inch twenty-yards "bull" can be substituted. This I think preferable to going back farther from the target as your skill increases; also it is safer, for the nearer the shooter is to the butt, the wider his shots would have to be for him to miss it; whereas, if he goes back to fifty yards he may easily shoot over a very high butt.

I am for the moment teaching "bull's-eye" shooting, but, as I ex-plain in my books on rifle shooting, I consider it preferable, if prac-ticable, instead of target shooting to shoot at an object which has no bull's-eye.

Place your empty pistol on the table, the weapon lying on its left side with the muzzle towards the target. The table is preferably a nar-row one, so that during the process of loading the pistol the muzzle points to the ground beyond the table and not at the table itself, an accidental discharge being thus immaterial. A table a foot wide is about right; the length does not matter provided the table be long enough to hold your glasses, cleaning implements, etc., and cartridges.

Position.—The position for shooting, which I am now going to describe, is one in which I shoot and the one which I have found from experience suits me best. This position, however, will have to be modified according to the build of the shooter (I am five feet ten inches tall, and weigh 168 pounds); a man stouter or shorter-necked than I am, might have to stand more sideways. I remember once, on the first day of a Bisley meeting, the non-commissioned officer in charge of my target saying: "Excuse me, sir, you are standing wrong."

I said: "What am I doing wrong? Show me."

He took my revolver—it was empty (I had been merely looking along the sights at the target to see if they needed blacking)—and showed me the regulation, conventional position—right side to the target, right arm bent, head and neck bent down to look along the sights, little finger under end of stock, etc. The position he showed me not only cramps one, strains the eyes (from having to look "round the corner" to the right) , and prevents one from being able to shoot at moving objects, but in addition one is very apt to be hit in the face by the revolver from the recoil of a heavy charge. A beginner almost invariably stands in this awkward, sideways position; it is also the conventional position with all artists, just as raising the right arm in jumping a fence. I suppose the origin of it is the conventional duelling position—trying to give your opponent a narrow target to aim at—but this is wrong even for duelling, as I explain in the chapter on that subject. From the shape of some men's figures, though, I am of opinion that there are men who would present a narrower mark—especially in the region of the belt—when facing an enemy! But this is a digression.

Stand facing the target, the right foot pointing straight for the target, or perhaps a shade to the left (if the ground be slippery this gives you a firmer foothold); the left heel distant from six to nine inches to the left of the right foot, according to your height (my distance is eight inches), and about an inch farther back; the feet turned out about as much as is natural to you when standing. Nails in the boots, or corrugated rubber, give a firmer hold, especially in short, dry grass.

Stand perfectly upright, not craning your head forward; the left arm should hang down straight, and close to the side, in the position

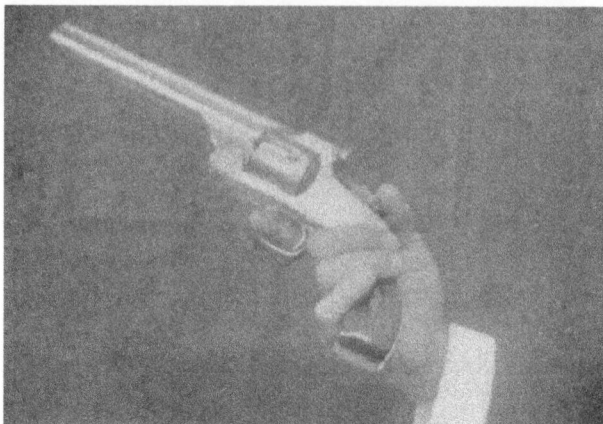

HOW TO COCK A REVOLVER

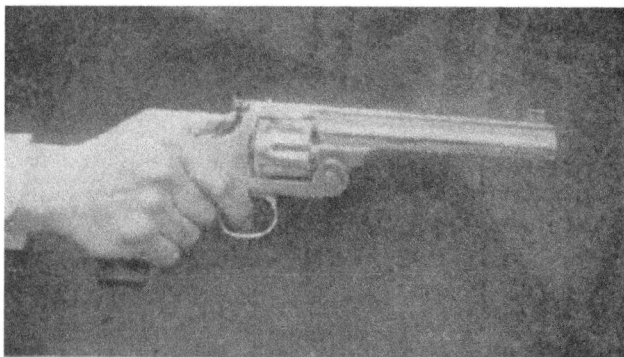

THE CORRECT WAY TO HOLD A REVOLVER

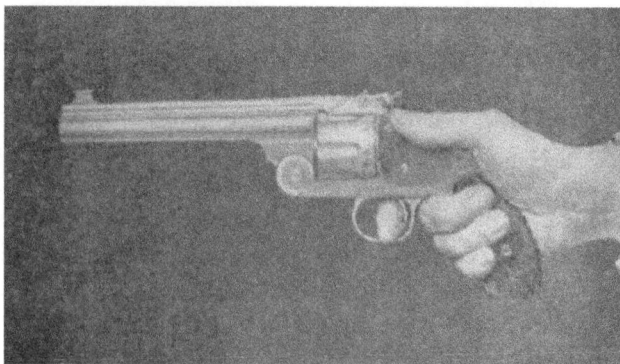

THE CORRECT POSITION OF THE THUMB

of "Attention." Some people bend the left arm and rest the hand on the hip; but I think this looks affected, and it is not as workmanlike as if the arm hangs straight down.

If you are trying to "hold" an especially important shot, and find yourself wobbling off your aim, it is a help to grip your thigh hard with your left hand; this especially applies in a gusty wind.

Now lift the pistol with your right hand (the weapon is empty, remember) and cock it. There are two ways of cocking: one using both hands and one using only the shooting hand. I do not refer to the double-action cocking by pulling back the trigger for the moment.

This single-handed cocking is done by putting the thumb on the hammer, and by the action of the thumb muscles alone bringing it to full-cock. Take particular care that the first finger is clear of the trigger, or else you will either break or injure the sear notch, or have an accidental "let-off." With practice, this way of cocking becomes very easy, and can be done with great rapidity. I personally can also let the pistol down to half-cock (manipulating it with one hand, with the trigger finger and thumb); but I would not advise a beginner to try this, except with an empty pistol, and even then only with one that he does not mind the chance of spoiling, as he is very apt to break the nose of the sear if he bungles it.

By practice, the thumb and forefinger muscles (*abductor pollicis* and *adductor indicis*) develop enormously, so you need not mind if at first this work of cocking seems difficult; but stop as soon as the muscles feel tired, or you may strain them. Pistol shooting is good also for the flexors of the forearm and for the dorsal muscles. A small hammer with short "fall" is easiest to cock, as well as to make good shooting with, for such a hammer takes less time in falling, and the aim is, in consequence, less likely to be disturbed.

The beginner will find that it assists the cocking to give the pistol a slight tilt to the right and upwards, taking great care to bring it back with the hind sight *horizontal* afterwards, as holding the sights tilted is one of the chief causes of bad shooting.

In double-handed cocking, assist the right hand by taking the revolver behind the chambers with the left hand, so as not to get burnt if it should go off by accident; with a pistol it is handier to grip farther forward; keep the barrel horizontal and pointed at the target, *not* (if you are competing) towards your left-hand neighbour, as is often done; and, while it is thus steadied, cock the revolver gently, not with a jerk, bringing the hammer well beyond full-cock, so that it sinks back into the bent with a well-defined "click," keeping the first finger clear of the trigger.

Now, stand with the pistol in your right hand, just back clear of the table; right arm full stretch; thumb stretched out along the revolver (see illustration), but the first finger must be outside the trigger-guard (*not touching the trigger*) during this stage. The duelling pistol has to be held differently, as will be seen in that chapter.

Some Englishmen shoot with the second finger on the trigger and the first along the revolver; but this is a clumsy way, and the first finger is apt to be burnt with the escape of gas from the cylinder. I have never seen men of any other nation do this. The habit was acquired from shooting the Martini rifle, the clumsy "grip" of which made this manner of holding necessary.

The great thing is to have your grip *as high as you* can on the stock, in line with the axis of the barrel, or as near this as is practicable. With the Smith & Wesson Russian Model I have it is as shown in the diagrams, actually in line with the bore of the barrel.

Some American revolvers for the British market often have specially long, big handles, or stocks, because of the habit (or is it the Regulation Position?) of holding the stock low down with the little finger beneath, prevalent in England. Now, this sort of position makes the recoil come at an angle to the wrist, throws the barrel up at the recoil, spoiling the accuracy, and puts more strain on the wrist than is necessary. I remember a very strong-wristed man firing one of my heavily charged fifty-yards revolvers and, owing to holding it in this way, spraining his wrist at the first shot; yet I have fired hundreds of rapid-firing shots straight on end with it without hurting myself. I take the recoil just as a man catches a hard-thrown ball, letting arm, hand, and wrist fly up all together.

The pistol-barrel, hand, and arm should all be nearly in one line, the thumb along the left side, so as to prevent jerking to the left in pressing the trigger (in the same way as the left arm is fully extended in shooting with the shotgun), and not crooked, as all beginners insist on holding it.

You must be constantly on the watch that you do not crook your thumb, until the extended position becomes second nature to you. Some makes of revolvers have the extractor lever in a position which renders this grip with extended thumb impossible, and then it has to be held with the "duelling grip." This applies also to most double-action revolvers.

For the benefit of beginners who are not target rifle-shots, the following explanation may be necessary. The target, for the convenience of locating shot-holes, is supposed to represent the face of a clock. The top of the bull's-eye (which we term "bull" for brevity) is called 12 o'clock, as that is, of course, where the numeral 12 appears on a clock face, and so on for all the other numerals: half-past four, for instance, is half-way between where the numerals 4 and 5 appear on a clock. I was once shooting in the presence of a German naval officer, and, when I made a "half-past four" "bull" shot, he said, "South-east," his professional instinct making him liken the target to the face of a compass.

First take a deep breath, and fill your lungs. Now slowly bring your right arm to the horizontal, keeping your eyes fixed on the bottom edge,—at "six o'clock" of the "bull;" whilst you are doing this, put your forefinger inside the trigger-guard, and gradually begin to feel the trigger and steadily increase the pressure on it *straight back, not sideways*. Whilst you are doing all this, also gradually stiffen all your muscles so that you are braced up, especially about the right shoulder, as though you were walking along the pavement and saw a man coming towards you whom you meant to shoulder out of your path.

You may breathe naturally until the revolver is levelled, then hold your breath; if you cannot get your aim satisfactorily before you feel you want to take a fresh breath, lower the pistol, take a deep breath, and try again. If you have followed these instructions carefully, you will find, when the hind sight comes to the level of your eyes (closing your left eye or not, as you find best, without any movement of the head), the front sight will be seen through the middle of the "U" pointed at the bottom of the bull's-eye, the top of the front sight just touching it at "six o'clock." If everything has been done perfectly, at the moment this occurs, the pressure on the trigger will have been increased sufficiently to cause the hammer to fall, and, after it has fallen, you will see the top of the front sight still just touching the bull's-eye at its bottom edge.

If the pistol had been loaded (assuming, of course, that it was an accurate-shooting one and properly sighted), you would have had a central bull's-eye for your shot. Most likely, however, you will find that the pistol came up all of a tremble, and that, as the hammer fell, the front sight was jerked to one side of the bull and perhaps even hidden by the hind sight.

Do not be discouraged, but cock the pistol and try again. By the way, it is best to have a "dummy" cartridge or an exploded one in the pistol whilst doing this "snapping" practice, as otherwise the jar may do damage to the pistol and perhaps break the main-spring. There are dummy cartridges, made with a rubber "buffer," for this practice. Preliminary practice with the duelling pistol is slightly different, and is explained later.

If you still find your hand shaky (and it is not naturally so), it most probably arises from your gripping too hard.

The action of "letting-off" should be like squeezing an orange—a squeeze of the *whole hand*. Start with a light grip when your hand is down, and gradually squeeze as you come up, the trigger-finger squeezing *back*; the hammer will then fall without your having the least tremor and without the sights moving off the point they covered during the fall of the hammer. The main thing of all in pistol shooting is to *squeeze straight back*. Whenever you find yourself shooting badly, see if you are not "*pulling off to one side*," or snatching; and in nine cases out of ten you will discover that this was the cause of your bad shooting.

Some men can never squeeze the trigger straight back, and have to allow for this by getting the hind sight "set over" to one side to correct it; but this is a slovenly way of shooting, and, as the pull to one side may vary according to the "jumpiness" of the shooter, it prevents his being a really first-class shot.

Keep the hind sight perfectly horizontal; beginners are prone to cant it on one side, which puts the bullet to the side towards which you cant.

After a little practice you will be able to "call" your shots, that is to say, you will be able, the moment the cartridge explodes, to say where the shot has struck the target, as you will know where the sights were pointed at the moment of the "squeeze-off."

After six shots, make a pencil-cross over each bullet-hole, so as to know where your former shots hit. After twelve hits it is best to take a fresh target. At the end of the day's shooting you can cover the holes by pasting black patches on the bull's-eye holes and white on the rest, and use the target again.

I will now say why I insist upon the importance of a table being set before the shooter. The usual procedure for a beginner with the pistol is this: He cocks the pistol, using both hands, pointing it at the spectators on his left whilst doing so; he then holds it with his right arm close to his side, pointing it towards the ground and at his right foot. He then brings it up with a flourish, high above his head, and lowers it to the target, jerks the trigger and "looses off." Of course he does not hit the target, but makes a very wild shot. After a few more shots on this principle, getting more and more wild, and making bigger flourishes with his pistol, he finally lets it off by accident whilst his arm is hanging by his side; and he is lucky if he does not make a hole in his right foot.

I remember a man once telling me (he professed to be an expert with the revolver) that I was wrong in keeping my revolver pointed in front of me towards the target when preparing to shoot. "You ought to hold it like this," he said, letting his right arm hang close to his side and keeping the revolver pointing downwards; "then it is quite safe." At that moment it went off and blew a big hole in the ground within an inch of his foot!

By my system of having a table in front of the shooter, close to which he stands, and from which he lifts the revolver, he cannot shoot down into his feet. But he must never turn round or leave the table without first unloading the revolver and placing it on the table; nor, on any account, must he let anyone go up to the target or be in front or even get level with him whilst the revolver is in his hand. In France one *must*, by the rules, keep the pistol pointed to the ground in competitions and *not* raise it from a table. But one learns not to point it at one's foot.

Now, as to the trick of lifting the revolver above one's head before firing: I *cannot* understand why people want to do this. It only frightens spectators; besides which the shooter is running the risk of shooting himself through the head; and in competitions or in self-defence time is too valuable to waste in such antics. What would be thought in covert-shooting of a man doing "Indian-club exercises" with his gun before firing each shot? Just as, when you see a man wet the point of his pencil with his lips, you know that he cannot draw, so, if a man flourishes his revolver, you may wager that he cannot shoot.

I have often been asked, "How do you shoot your revolver? Do you bring it up or down on your object?"

I reply: "What is the use of lifting it up above your head merely to bring it down again?"

For self-defence, you take it out of your pocket or holster; in competitions you take it from the table; in duelling you bring it up from your thigh. In all cases it is brought up from the level of your hips or lower. Why, then, should you lift it above your head and lower it again? No; *bring it up straight on the object by the shortest and quickest route.* In a case of self-defence, you would have your man down before he had finished flourishing his revolver round his head.

When you are pretty confident that you can keep your sights properly aligned at the bottom edge of the bull while the hammer is falling, you can try a few shots with a loaded pistol. It is best to load only some of the chambers, and irregularly if using a revolver,—that is to say spin the cylinder round, after the revolver is closed and at half-cock, so as not to know which chambers are loaded, and, every time you find you jerk off a shot, return to the snapping-empty-cartridges practice. This latter is good practice, even when you become a finished shot. I often have a few minutes of snapping practice in my room.

Place the box of cartridges beside, and to the right of, the pistol. Use only a very small charge (gallery ammunition for choice, or the .22 short in the single-shot pistol) at first, as nothing puts a beginner off so much as the fear of recoil. Stand behind the table, the revolver being between you and the target, and take the revolver by its stock in the right hand. Do not turn the muzzle to the left, but keep it straight towards the target. Put the revolver in your left hand, then load it. This proedure varies with different makes; with the Smith & Wesson Russian and Winans revolvers you lift the catch with your left thumb and press the barrel down with the same hand till it (the barrel) is perpendicular, pointing to the ground. With the Colt, and with the Smith & Wesson solid frame revolver, you push the catch and then push the chamber out to the side. But, whatever the mechanism, the barrel should be pointing downward when the revolver is open for loading, yet in line with the target.

If a cartridge projects too much, remove it, it is dangerous as it may explode prematurely from friction against the breech of the revolver. In loading of course have the pistol at half-cock, and not at full-cock. Close it by elevating the breech with the right hand, and not by raising the barrel with the left, as in the latter case the cartridges may drop out. This rule applies also to the hand-ejecting revolvers; two types of action are here illustrated. Another is the Colt solid frame, where a gate opens and the cartridges are put in, revolving the cylinder as each cartridge is inserted. When this revolver is loaded see that the snap, or other fastening, is properly closed. If your shot goes wide of the bull, be sure, before you alter your aim for the next shot, to ascertain whether it was not your "squeeze-off" that was to blame.

A practised shot can correct the shooting of his revolver by "aim-ing-off" enough to rectify any error in sights. But the beginner had better not attempt this: he will find enough to do in trying to hold straight under the bull.

TWO SYSTEMS OF EJECTING SMITH & WESSON

Do not mind if your score is not a high one; those who do not understand shooting judge the goodness of a score by how much it counts, or by how many shots are in or near the bull's-eye. In reality, it is the *group* which constitutes a good shoot. One score may consist of the highest possible,—forty-two points (all six shots bull's-eyes),—and another may only count twelve points; and yet the latter may be by far the better "shoot."

I will explain. In the first case the shots may be "all over" the bull, "nicking" the edges; they would require, therefore, a circle of more than four inches (on the target you are at present shooting at) to cover them. The other score may consist of all six bullet-holes cut-ting into each other at an extreme edge of the target, but making a group which could be covered with a postage-stamp. The first "shoot" is a wild, bad shoot for ten yards' range at a four-inch bull, although it counts the highest possible in conventional scoring. The other is a magnificent shoot, one that anyone might be proud of; the fact of its being up in the corner merely showing that the sights were wrong, and the shooter's "holding" was not to blame.

A few touches of the file, or knocking over the hind sight, will put this error right. Never mind, therefore, about scoring many points; merely shoot for *group*. You will gradually find your groups getting smaller and smaller as you improve; it is then merely a matter of filing to get good scoring.

As your four-inch bull's-eye is too large for real shooting at ten yards, you must remember that the sighting of the pistol should put the bullets into *one inch only* in this size bull at "6 o'clock," and not into the middle of it. The reason is that the trajectory of a pistol is practically the same at twenty as at ten yards; and, as the English regulation bull at twenty yards is two inches, for revolver shooting you want the twenty-yards sighted revolver to put the shots into the centre of the two-inch bull when you aim at the bottom edge. In other words, you want it to shoot an inch higher than your aim at that distance. Therefore, if with your four-inch "Bull," aiming at the bottom edge, you go into the bull one inch up, it means a central bull's-eye if shot on a two-inch bull.

In France an inch bull at sixteen metres is regulation, so, if practising for French competitions, the pistol must shoot only half an inch into the bull. The reason I recommend aiming at the bottom of the bull's-eye instead of at the middle of it is that if you try to put a black bead in the middle of a black bull's-eye you cannot see either properly; while if you whiten the bead of the fore sight you cannot see it clearly against the white of the target in "coming up" to the bull. Nobody can hold *absolutely* steady on the bull for more than a fraction of a second; you have to "come up" from below and "squeeze off" as you get your sights aligned.

For *real* shooting—I mean at game, or in self-defence, or in war—a white sight is best, as it shows more clearly against the objects most likely to be met with. It is for this reason that I think white targets are a mistake for practical revolver practice.

In France you *must* use a white metal front sight. This is all right on the black "man" target, but it is bad for the bull's-eye target. The French, however, lay more stress on "real" shooting than on target shooting.

If you want to learn pistol shooting for practical purposes only, and do not desire to compete for prizes, use, for the foregoing lessons, a black target with a white bull's-eye. Use a white front sight, and, as soon as you become moderately proficient, take to practising at moving, disappearing, rapid-firing, traversing, advancing and retiring targets, directions for which I give under their proper heads in my Bisley chapters. Take care, however, instead of Bisley targets to have *black* targets with white bull's-eyes at first and then dispense with the "bull" and shoot for centre hits, using a white front sight.

In all your shooting *take a full sight in a widely open "U," so that you see daylight all round the front sight.* This is the only way to get quick aim in all lights. A finer sight may do for target-potting in bright sunlight, in deliberate shooting at a stationary target, but it is useless for practical purposes. Unless you want to be a winner of prizes for that style of shooting do very little shooting at stationary targets.

It is best to have your cleaning appliances on the table, or otherwise handy, as in a drawer, when shooting, and every now and again to take a look through the barrel and then give the barrel a wipe out; otherwise you may be inclined to attribute to bad shooting what is in reality caused by leading or by hard fouling in the barrel. I have a little cupboard under my table, with a lock and key to it, in which I keep my cleaning apparatus, cartridges, etc. (but *not* the pistol) , in order to save the trouble of carrying all this paraphernalia to the range.

With the French smokeless powder, however, cleaning during shooting is unnecessary, though the cylinder of a revolver may occasionally need a little oil.

Always clean a revolver as soon as possible after shooting with it, and clean thoroughly.

A revolver shows signs of wear first at the breech end of the barrel, when it gets to look as though rats had been gnawing at it there. I am inclined to think that at first this makes the revolver shoot "sweeter," but when it gets too bad it affects the accuracy of the weapon for target work. For real work, I prefer a revolver when it is half worn out, as everything then works smoothly and there is less danger of jamming. But rust in the rifling may entirely spoil accuracy, as, if you work it off, the bore gets enlarged and then the bullets "strip." I never like to compete with a perfectly new revolver; all revolvers have their peculiarities, and it is necessary to get used to one, to "break it in," so to speak, before trusting it to obey one's slightest hint.

Details for target-shooting, in competition, at a fifty-yards' stationary target, I treat of in the proper place in the Bisley chapters. I do not see much use in practising at the regulation four-inch bull at fifty yards for improving one's shooting for practical purposes. The bull is too small for the accuracy of a revolver and for sighting on, and causes one to get slow and "polly;" also fifty yards is not a revolver distance, it is a .22 pistol distance.

When the present Bisley targets were designed (I was one of the committee), it was decided to have a two-inch bull at twenty yards. It will be noticed that I have since modified my opinion and that I now think it ought to be smaller for a twenty-yards stationary target; but I consider, nevertheless, that it is about right for moving targets. I then suggested five inches as right for the bull at fifty yards. It was, however, decided to make it four inches, which I thought then, and still think, much too small.

If two inches be right for twenty yards, five inches is the rule-of-three proportion for fifty yards. The barrel of a revolver is so short, and the sights are so close together, that the four-inch bull is too small for the "natural error" of holding of even the best of shots. The longer single-shot pistol is a different matter, and the strength of the shots does not vary from escape of gas at the chambers as it does in revolvers.

For practice at fifty yards and over, for practical purposes, you should have a white bull on a black ground, six or seven inches in diameter at fifty yards, and a foot in diameter at a hundred yards. Use the same big, coarse sights that you use at the shorter range, and aim high or low, according to distance, instead of raising the hind sight or using different revolvers sighted for special distances.

At Bisley, owing to the small bull and to the great accuracy required, very minute front sights have to be used. But I am talking of practical shooting; and at fifty yards, and over, a revolver would be used only to hit something at least as big as a deer.

At a hundred yards one ought to get into, or close to, a twelve-inch bull. Shooting, of a sort, in the standing position has been done up to four hundred yards with a heavy-charge revolver; but at more than a hundred yards one cannot depend on much accuracy and can only use the revolver for "browning." I have shot at one-hundred-and-ten yards at the "running deer" at Bisley with the revolver, but it is too far to do much good. At fifty yards, at the "deer," one can do really good shooting and get three shots into it in one of its runs. Fifty yards I consider a good distance at which to make sure of a crossing horse, galloping, and one hundred yards for a standing one.

In all competitions the revolver must be held in one hand only, although one sees so-called "dead shots" on the stage hold their pistols with both hands. The revolver can be held steadier by some people when both hands are used, the hand which does not hold the stock being rested against a tree, or other rest, and the barrel of the revolver clasped to steady it, much as a telescope is held. The left hand may also clasp the right wrist, or *vice versa*. Another way is to clasp the shooting arm with the other hand and rest the revolver below the biceps muscles; but a heavily charged revolver is apt in this position to strike the face. Moreover this style of shooting is about upon a par with holding on to a horse's mane, or to the pommel of the saddle, and calling it riding.

Lying on the back and resting the revolver alongside one of your knees, the legs being crossed, is a very steady position. Sitting down with the arms folded, and shooting off one arm, is another steady position.

Never leave a pistol, loaded or unloaded, where anyone can touch it. Keep it locked up, unless actually in your own possession.

One of my ornamental revolvers used to lie as a decoration on the writing-table in my Bisley hut. Of course it was unloaded, and there were no cartridges near. Some visitors chanced to drop in, one by one, to lunch.

First came an elderly lady. She sat down near the table and her eye fell on the revolver. Instantly she snatched it up, and pointed it straight at me, exclaiming with a laugh, "I'll shoot you!" I made her put it down, and was explaining to her how unwise it is to point a revolver at anyone, how it might have been loaded, and so on, when in came a parson. He sat down and began talking pleasantly. Presently he caught sight of the revolver. Grabbing it, he shouted: "Now then, I'll shoot you!" and he too pointed it at me, roaring with laughter. Carlyle's famous remark about the world's population recurred to me, and I decided in future to keep the revolver locked up.

It is sometimes useful to be able to shoot with the left hand; as, for instance, if the right hand should become disabled, and for an officer with a sword in his right hand the advantage would be considerable. If the novice has determination enough to divide his practising, *from the beginning*, between both hands, he will come to shoot nearly as well with his "left" hand as with his right. I have put quotation marks round "left," as I mean by this the hand not usually employed; a left-handed man's right hand being in this sense his "left."

I have also noticed that a left-handed man can shoot more evenly with both hands; that is to say, he is not much better or much worse with either hand, not being so helpless with his right hand as a normally handed man is with his left. In all directions given for shooting, for left-handed work merely change "right leg" to "left leg"; "right arm" to "left arm," and so on.

CHAPTER 9

Practice and Training

What amount of practice is necessary in order to keep a man at his best, varies in different people. It is evident that he cannot be always at his best, any more than he can at all times be in perfect condition for any other class of contest, athletic or otherwise. If he tried to become so he would only become "stale."

If you are going to shoot in a competition, do your preliminary work so that you come to your best at the time you need it, and *not before*, as so many do. Some practise so that they are shooting their best some time prior to the event for which they are training, and then they get "stale" and go off their shooting just when they want to shoot well. It is the better plan to be hardly at one's best when the competition opens, but to be "coming on."

Get into as good general health as you can. Take a dose of something which acts upon the liver, if needful. You cannot shoot well if your liver be not in perfect order. Shoot very little at first. Gradually do more and more every day; but slacken, or even stop, for a day or two if you find you are overdoing it. Stop smoking if you are a smoker; and be very abstemious in what you drink. Personally, I have been a water drinker and a non-smoker all my life.

Some men, like myself, can never do as good work in practice as when entered for an uphill competition that will need to be hard fought. They need the stimulus of competing to wake them up. I do not remember ever making so good a score in practice as I have done in competition, except one single score at rapid firing. With some, a hard tussle, instead of making them pull themselves together and bracing them up, has just the opposite effect; they go all to pieces when "pushed" or in a tight place. I am afraid such men can never do any good in shooting competitions. To win, a man, like a trotting horse, should, as Ira Paine used to say, have a little "devil" in him. If a man is "soft," or too good-natured and easy-going, and of a "never-mind" disposition, he is no good in shooting competitions; while on the other hand if he be excitable or irascible he will "get shaking" and upset himself just when he ought to keep cool. Some even brood over a coming match until, when the struggle commences, their nerves are all unstrung. Others again work themselves into a fever of excitement by exclamations of impatience each time a shot or anything else goes wrong.

When getting ready for an important shoot, I begin some months before, shooting *once* on each day and then *dismissing from my mind for the rest of the day all thought of shooting*. Gradually I work it up to an hour and a half daily, during which time I fire from two hundred to four hundred shots. For an average man this is too many shots a day. Three days before the time, I stop shooting, so as to come fresh to it and avoid being "stale;" but some men find it better to work right up to the day itself.

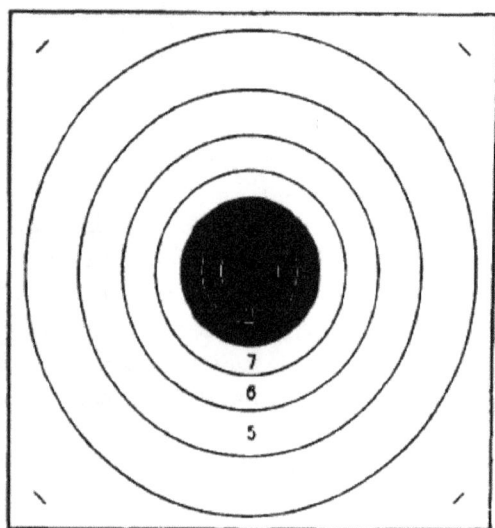

STANDARD AMERICAN TARGET
Diameter of Circles

10 circle	. . 3.36 inches	} Bull's-eye	6 circle	. . 14.80 inches
9 "	. . 5.54 "		5 "	. . 19.68 "
8 "	. . 8.00 "		4 "	. . 26.00 "
7 "	. . 11.00 "			

Rest of target 28 × 28 inches

You ought not to shoot quite alone; I mean you ought to have a competitor and an audience, and, if possible, a hostile (or feignedly hostile) one. It is advisable to get people to stand behind you and make remarks about your shooting; laughing when you make a bad shot; telling each other anecdotes (this latter is very disconcerting; the former only makes you set your teeth and shoot all the better), and occasionally letting something drop with a bang, just at a critical moment in your shooting.

This will accustom you to shoot in competition before spectators, and prevent your becoming disconcerted by their presence. I do not mean to say that you will be so treated at Bisley or at the clubs, for the range officers at Bisley are very strict in making anyone who is not shooting stand well back and not talk loudly, and in France the strictest etiquette is observed in this connection. But with the above training you will come not to mind even a buzz of conversation and movement behind you when you are competing, or, indeed, the sudden silence which denotes that you are about to fire a shot on which much depends. Had you, however, practised always in solitude, you would, when shooting in public, be far less composed and self-possessed.

I think that anyone who is really an expert pistol shot can, *for a few shots*, shoot well at any time (when in normal health), without any practice. Once I did not have a pistol in my hand for nearly a year, and then I made a highest possible score at my first attempt. But one cannot keep it up for any number of shots, the muscles being out of training and the thumb and trigger-finger getting sore, and even cut.

Be careful when training not to get a "raw" or sprain anywhere on your shooting hand; if you feel one coming, rest that hand till it is healed, and gradually you will get a "corn" where the friction existed. If you shoot with a "raw" you will be liable to flinch, and so find it harder to shoot in good form. I shot all through one Bisley meeting with my right wrist sprained; and at another with my right thumb partly out of joint. But I had to keep on shooting, as my championship depended on winning. There is one great charm of the Pistolet Club, and all pistol shooting in France; you shoot with light charges and so do not get knocked about, and deafened, as you do in England where one is compelled to use heavy charges. If only for this reason I think that pistol shooting will never become popular in England under existing rules.

In reference to practice not being necessary to a seasoned shot, it is much better not to have practised at all than to be "stale." I remember one of the best shots at the "running deer" range telling me he never took a rifle in his hand except during the Wimbledon fortnight (we used in those days to have the N.R.A. at Wimbledon); but then he was always using a gun the rest of the year, and this was better practice than using a rifle at stationary targets, hence perhaps his invariable success in beating the target shots.

On a wet, windy, or otherwise unsuitable day, it is best to keep entirely away from open-air pistol ranges. You will not have wasted time; you will, most likely, do better shooting the next time; and the others will probably all be "shot out" without having anything to show for it.

Above all things, do not stand behind a good shot and watch him beating your best score; this is fatal to your nerves.

It is advisable to have a good leather case, with a lock, and your name on it, for your ammunition at Bisley. If you use the ammunition from the boxes in which the cartridges are sold, you are very apt to find yourself using someone else's cartridges by mistake—often bad ones. I recollect an orderly at one Bisley meeting collecting all the odd lots of revolver-cartridges lying about the firing-points. He placed them in a box, *and a competitor used them by mistake!*

BADGES WON BY THE AUTHOR

CHAPTER 10

Gallery Shooting

By this term I mean shooting under cover as distinct from shooting in the open air.

Some people say of gallery shooting, "This is not sport," just as those who have never tried "tame deer" and "drag" hunting say that *these* are not sport. One can, however, get a lot of fun out of both, under circumstances in which anything that people call "legitimate" sport would be impossible.

Nobody can make good shooting with a pistol in a wind. When I say this, I am generally told: "You *ought* to be *able* to shoot in any weather." I do not mind shooting a match in a gale of wind if my adversary is also exposed to it, as that is good sport. But, I repeat, it is impossible, except by a fluke, to make a really good score in a wind, or to do any shooting which is useful as practice. You may shoot hard all day long whenever a wind is blowing, and, instead of improving your shooting, it will entirely spoil your "form" and "timing." The reason is this: With a rifle, especially if you use the "back" position, you can "hold" steady in quite a strong wind, and the wind only lends interest and brings science into play in "allowing for wind." With the pistol, on the contrary, you have to stand up, the wind blows your arm and body about, you have only one arm to steady the pistol, and that is being buffeted about at full stretch. How would you shoot if someone took hold of the sleeve of your shooting arm and kept twitching it as you tried to aim, and at the same time pushed you? This is what the wind practically does.

As it is impossible to shoot to any advantage in a wind, the summer months are generally the only ones when pistol competitions are practicable in the open air. A pistol-shot cannot get any practice out-of-doors on boisterous winter days, especially if he is busy all day

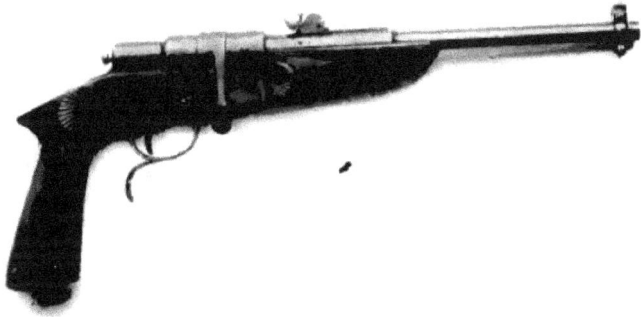

BELGIAN SINGLE-SHOT PISTOL.—SAW-HANDLE

BELGIAN SINGLE-SHOT PISTOL. SAW-HANDLE
Showing breech open

and the light fails just at the time he is free. This is when the indoor gallery comes in useful.

I do not know of any good public pistol-shooting gallery in England at the present moment, although there are several clubs where heavy charges are shot and where no light trigger-pull is allowed, or light charges. In Paris, Gastinne-Renette's, 39, Avenue d'Antin, is furnished with all the latest modern improvements and it has the *very great* advantage that the shooting is by daylight and in the open air and sheltered from the wind. There is at the Gastinne-Renette Gallery an annual competition during March, April, and May, with prize pistols, revolvers, and medals. For ordinary practice, the revolver subscription is at the rate of 55*f.* per 500 shots, or 30*f.* per 250 shots. I will give fuller details of the matches shot there in my chapter on the duelling pistol, and some particulars about the light charges.

A private gallery can easily be fitted up in the cellars of large country houses, or even of town houses. All that is needed is a gallery of moderate length—ten yards will suffice at a pinch, though in mine it is possible to shoot up to thirty-three yards—with targets and butt.

The targets should be lighted from above, in daytime preferably by a skylight, and by gas lamps or electric lights at night. When artificial light is used, it should be screened, so that from the firing-point the targets are distinct and the source of the light is invisible. At the firing-point it is difficult to get a satisfactory light at night. If this gallery is not made in a green-house, which, of course, would give ample light to sight by in the day, I think there is no use in trying to get the light to shine on your sights at night. If it is behind you, you stand in your own light. If enough above you to prevent this, the light only shines on the top edges of your sights, and is thus worse than useless. I find it best to have enough light behind me to enable me to load, etc., and to trust to seeing the sights in a black silhouette against the target. You may, for this reason, have to alter your sights from the elevation which suits you out-of-doors.

You should have a ventilating shaft straight above the muzzle of your revolver, and, if possible, a fan to draw off the fumes and smoke; this can be worked by electricity or by water-power.

It is expedient to use only the lightest gallery ammunition, and it deadens the sound if you have the walls covered with some sort of thick material hung loosely. Boiler-felt is very good for the purpose. Also if you shoot through a hole in a partition screen it helps to deaden the sound.

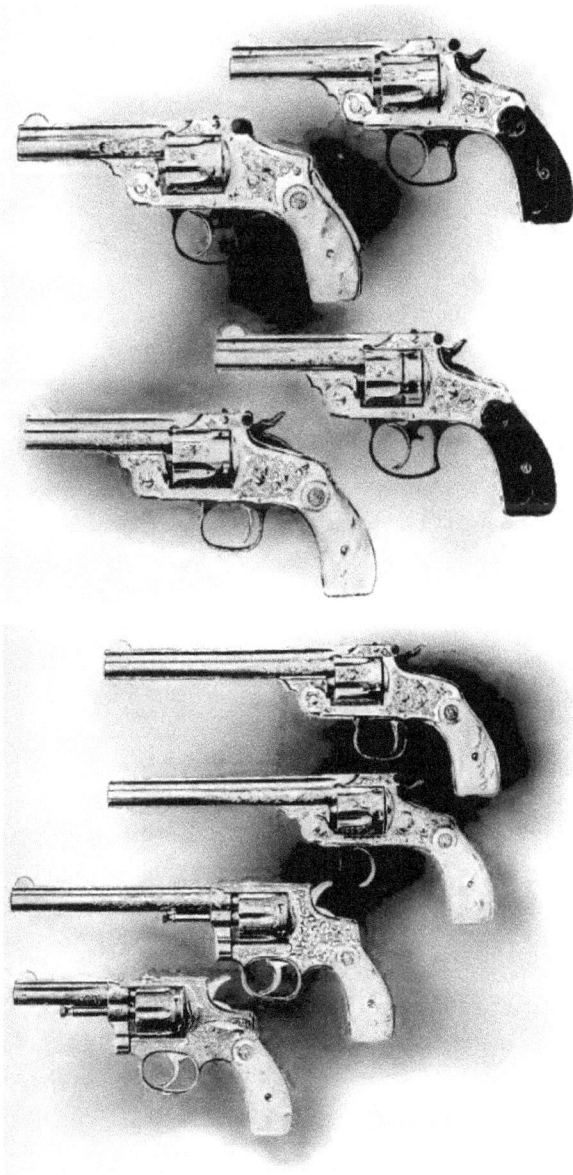

STYLES OF SMITH & WESSON ENGRAVING

I prefer a big-calibre revolver, as it gives a better chance to score; a shot which would be just out of the bull with a small bullet may just cut the bull with a large ball. The bullet-hole is also more easily seen, but the bullet must be round so as to be as light as possible or you will have to use too heavy a charge of powder to propel it.

The self-registering targets, such as are used for miniature .22 calibre rifles, I do not find very satisfactory at ranges under 20 yards; those, at least, that I have tried; the larger size of the revolver bullet makes it liable to strike two compartments at the same time, giving you a double score. The impact of the bullet is, moreover, too heavy for the mechanism. I prefer card targets for short ranges, and at 25 yards Gastinne-Renette's self-registering targets. Do not have targets that necessitate anyone's going down the range, or coming out from a mantlet, to change. Have the card targets made to draw up to the firing-point for examination and change, and never let anyone turn round with a revolver in his hand. In fact, observe all the rules as to table to fire from, etc., which I give in the chapter on Learning to Use the Pistol. All these rules apply equally to gallery shooting.

As the gallery is generally narrow, it may be difficult to have traversing targets, but you can have disappearing or rapid-firing at my cinematograph targets.

Such a gallery will be an endless source of amusement in the winter evenings, after dinner; and the ladies can shoot as well as the men.

It is advisable to handicap the good shots, so as to give all an equal chance.

I have lately devised a cinematograph target that should afford good practice, especially in ranges where miniature small-arms are used.

According to my invention I provide a plain target, preferably painted white, and I project on to the same by means of cinematograph apparatus representations of animals or men running and doubling across the surface of the target.

The target is so constructed and arranged in connection with the cinematograph apparatus that when struck by the bullet the traverse of the cinematograph film will be momentarily arrested so that the representation remains stationary on the target. During this brief period while the film is stationary it will be possible to see the result of the shot. The travel of the film will then be resumed and the practice may continue.

The target may be of any suitable material and may be made in several separately mounted parts if desired so as to more readily respond to the impact of the shot and arrest the film.

It is obvious that a much greater variety of running and moving objects may be provided for shooting practice by means of the cinematograph than can be afforded by the mechanism usually employed for providing moving targets.

Gallery shooting is by far the most scientific style of revolver shooting, if you use a very light load, fine sights, and hair trigger; therefore you can have smaller bull's-eyes and subdivisions than the Bisley ones. The American and the French targets are better subdivided for this purpose. Messrs. De La Rue make me special "ace of hearts" packs of cards for use as targets, also one with a blue-bottle fly as a bull's-eye, natural size. Also for experimental work a gallery is much more reliable than shooting out-of-doors.

When shooting with gallery ammunition in which the bullets are "seated" low, look into the cartridges before putting them into the chambers, as a bullet may have worked itself up, which would cause a weak, low shot. Push the bullet down with a loading rod, or a pencil, before you insert the cartridge into the chamber, if you find the bullet has shifted. Also if for any reason after firing a few shots with this ammunition you stop, and want to reload the chambers which have been fired, it is as well to take out all the cartridges that have not been fired, and examine them, as the jar of firing may have started some of the bullets. They need re-seating.

If you can possibly get some of the French smokeless powder, as used at Gastinne-Renette's Gallery, this is much the best powder to use for this purpose, as it shoots evenly, does actually not make smoke, gives very little smell (and that not unpleasant), and shoots so "cleanly" that you can fire hundreds of shots without cleaning the pistol.

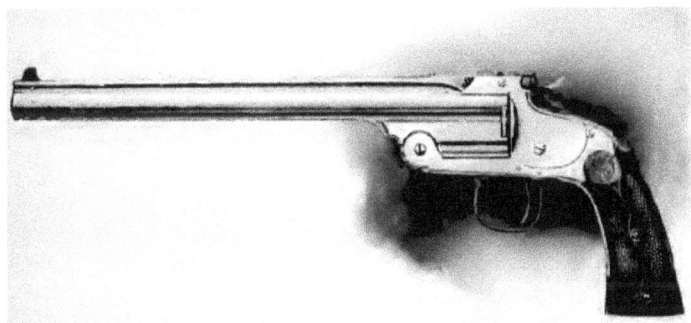

SMITH & WESSON SINGLE-SHOT TARGET PISTOL

71

Chapter 11

Gastinne-Renette's Gallery in Paris

THE DUELLING PISTOL

In regard to galleries where one can get pistol practice, that of
Gastinne-Renette in Paris stands easily first, as not only is it lit up in
the best style for all sorts of shooting, but the weapons supplied are the
best in the world. Founded in 1835, it has recently been refitted.

The usual shooting gallery in England is lit by artificial light, and
badly at that, and what in my opinion is the chief cause of English
galleries of this kind being so little patronised is that they are run on
the principle of "*All pay, nothing receive.*"

No matter how well you shoot,—you may, indeed, be beating all
the records in the world,—when you have done shooting you simply
pay so much for every shot you have fired, and get nothing in return.

Naturally a man soon gets tired of this, and, so far as practice is con-
cerned, it is better and comes far cheaper to fix up a private range.

At Gastinne-Renette's, on the contrary, if you make a good score
you receive a gold, a silver, or a bronze medal, or plaque, or an *objet
d'art* is given to you, while in addition your score is inscribed in a
permanent register. When the target is an exceptionally good one it
is framed and set up in the gallery, your name being inscribed in gold
letters in the "Roll of Honour" on a slab on the wall.

There are scores there that have been made by almost all the best
pistol-shots in the world who have visited the gallery at various times.
They date, I believe, from seventy years back. There are some very
good scores by the late King of Portugal.

Also you can subscribe for practice, and then your shooting costs
very little.

While there are plenty of competitions and medals to be won at deliberate shooting, most of the shooters prefer the more practical practice of rapid firing.

I suppose it is a matter of national temperament. Again, whilst in England it is the hardest thing possible to get men to shoot at anything but stationary targets and do deliberate shooting, either in rifle or revolver competitions (they have no pistol competitions), in France it is the minority who go for deliberate shooting. Very many go in for the rapid-shooting competitions with pistol and revolver.

In consequence, whilst one could count on the fingers of one hand all the Englishmen who can shoot well at moving targets or who are expert in rapid firing with a revolver, in Paris there are several dozen very brilliant shots, over and above plenty who can shoot really well.

I do not remember ever seeing at Gastinne-Renette's the name of an Englishman who had won even a bronze medal in the rapid-firing or moving-object competitions, and the only American name there is my own.

If anyone, therefore, wants to become a first-class pistol-or revolver-shot I would strongly recommend him to do his practising at Gastinne-Renette's.

The gallery, warmed by hot water pipes in winter, has a series of openings into the outer air, in which the shooters and their assistants stand. These being shut off by glass doors from the main gallery, spectators can watch the shooting without their being annoyed by the noise of the reports. The targets stand out in the open court.

The shooting is all done with light charges and with a light trigger-pull—unless otherwise specially desired, in which case one can get knocked to pieces and half deafened by shooting with heavy charges in a gallery beneath.

In none of the competitions is one forced to use heavy charges or a heavy trigger-pull, and this makes the shooting far more enjoyable. The heavy trigger-pull obligatory in England has caused many a man to discontinue revolver shooting, for this heavy pull requires a lifetime to master. And when it is mastered it is of no earthly-use, as no man in his senses would use a heavy trigger-pull if his life depended upon his skill in shooting.

As this chapter deals with the duelling pistol, I will begin by describing how this weapon is used in practice. In a subsequent chapter I will explain how it is used in an actual duel.

The duelling pistol is a single-shot muzzle-loader of .40 calibre.

The best make is Gastinne-Renette's. He makes two other sorts of

GASTINNE-RENETTE'S
GALLERY

UNDERGROUND GALLERY
FOR HEAVY CHARGES

GASTINNE-RENETTE'S
GALLERY—FIRING POINTS

breech-loading duelling pistols as well, but as the muzzle-loader is the regulation duelling pistol, I will describe it first.

It has, as will be seen by the illustration, a straighter grip than a revolver, also it has a spur on the trigger-guard.

One way of holding it is to put the second finger round this spur (see fig. 1), but most of the best shots hold it as in fig. 2.

Whilst for a revolver I advocate holding the thumb along the top of the grip (as explained in Chapter 8), the stock is too straight for this hold with the duelling pistol, and the thumb must therefore be turned down, as shown in fig. 4 (also in fig. 3).

How far you hold up the stock must be determined by practice. If you hold very high up, and you have a muscular or fat hand, the flesh between your thumb and forefinger will hide your hind sight. Hold it as high up as possible, however, and do not get too much of the forefinger round the trigger; also remember to squeeze straight back.

The assistant—you are not allowed to load your own weapon or to shoot without an assistant being with you—loads the pistol as follows:

He has, on the ledge before him, a bowl of smokeless powder, a bowl of caps, and a bowl of round bullets.

He first puts on a cap and snaps it, to clear the nipple (generally a pair of pistols are used, he loading the one whilst you shoot the other); then he puts in, with a small scoop, a load of powder; and lastly he puts on a cap. All this time the pistol has been kept "muzzle up," to prevent the powder from running out. This charge of powder he also shoots off to clear the nipple. Now the pistol is ready for loading.

He puts in the powder, then puts a bullet on the muzzle, taps it down with a wooden mallet, and then drives it home with a wooden loading rod and the mallet.

Next he puts on a cap, and then he hands you the pistol at half cock, his thumb on the cap.

There are two distances for the duelling pistol, namely sixteen metres and twenty-five metres; the former is for deliberate shooting, the latter is for rapid firing under duelling conditions.

A number of medals and plaques are offered to be shot for at both distances, either at targets, eggs, figures in plaster of Paris, plates, figures of running men or running rabbits, and, at the longer range, at the black silhouette of a life-sized man.

The bronze medals and plaques can be won by any moderately good shot; to win the silver medals needs very good shooting; and to

FIG. 1. HOW SOME HOLD THE DUELLING PISTOL

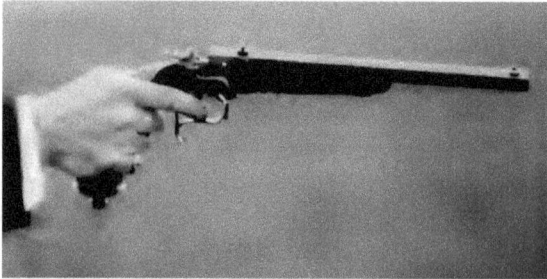

FIG. 2. THE AUTHOR'S WAY OF HOLDING THE DUELLING PISTOL

FIG. 3. HOW SOME HOLD THE DUELLING PISTOL (ANOTHER VIEW)

FIG. 4. THE AUTHOR'S WAY OF HOLDING THE DUELLING PISTOL
(ANOTHER VIEW)

secure the gold ones the competitor must be a brilliant marksman.

It will be found—at least I find it so—that in the deliberate shooting better scores can be made with a duel-ling pistol than with a revolver, and the scores that have won the gold medal with pistol and revolver respectively bear me out in this. I give at the end of this chapter details of what scores have to be made to win these various events.

As the special use of the duelling pistol, however, is for duelling, I will now describe how to become proficient with it in that style of shooting, leaving for a later chapter the points to be observed in an actual duel.

The metronome to beat 100 to the minute. You cock the pistol and stand with the left foot behind the line of the opening,—the right foot may be outside on the mat,—your elbow touching your hip, the butt of the pistol touching your thigh, and the pistol pointing at the ground.

Be very careful not to touch the trigger, as the pull is so light; be careful also not to point the muzzle at your right foot, for in that case you might put a bullet through your foot in the event of an accidental discharge.

The assistant, speaking at the speed of the metronome, says: "*Attention! Feu! Un—deux—trois!*" At the word "*feu*" you raise the pistol, which must be fired before the word "*trois.*" This is called shooting "*Au Commandement.*"

The target consists of a steel black figure of a man in profile (see figure) . The various parts count 5, 4, 3, and 2, respectively, the highest count being the oblong in the middle of the body, and the lowest, the legs. The head counts 3.

This figure is connected electrically with a small indication figure at the side of the firing-point, a bell ringing and a numbered disc appearing on the latter figure in the section struck by the bullet in the original.

The marker then goes out—after calling out "*plaque*" to ensure all being clear—and paints over the bullet mark.

This competition is shot very much on the lines of the "disappearing target" competition at Bisley, described later, and you had better read that chapter in connection with this one.

There are some differences, however.

Besides the grip and balance of the duelling pistol being different from those of the revolver, the pistol has to be raised from pointing to

SILHOUETTE SHOWING SPOTS MADE
BY THE AUTHOR IN COMPETITION
AT THE GASTINNE-RENETTE
GALLERY, APRIL 7, 1910

the ground, instead of from the hip level. This has a tendency to make you shoot low, as the time taken in raising the arm has to be hurried.

The sight is a shiny silver bead instead of a black one; the target has no visible "bull," and the divisions of the target have to be judged, as they do not show from the firing point.

It will be noticed that the middle oblong, counting five, is not absolutely central. The figure's chest projects to the right, and its waist comes in on the left side. If the figure were made of parallelograms you could judge the centre (horizontally) all the way up; but, with the shape it is, if you shoot for the centre of the bull you are apt to get out to the right as the "bull" is at that point to the left (*i.e.*, there is more inner on its right; and conversely, if you hit low for the bull you are apt to get an inner to the left). The best way is to come up a trifle to the left of the centre of the figure, otherwise you will spoil a "possible" by two or three inners on the right of the bull.

If you find, that you are shooting low it is much easier to hit the figure just below the bull than anywhere else, for which reason I have advised that place to shoot for in a real duel. One gets there so much

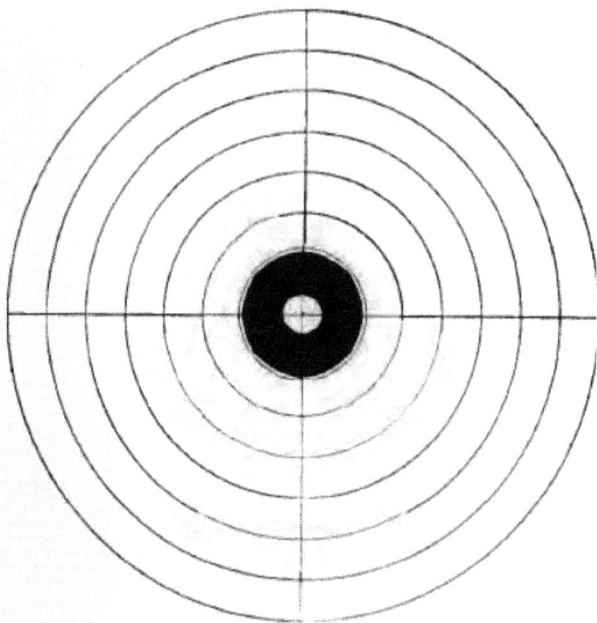

THE GASTINNE-RENETTE 16 METRES TARGET

This target has a $1\frac{3}{16}$ black. The ring is to facilitate judging

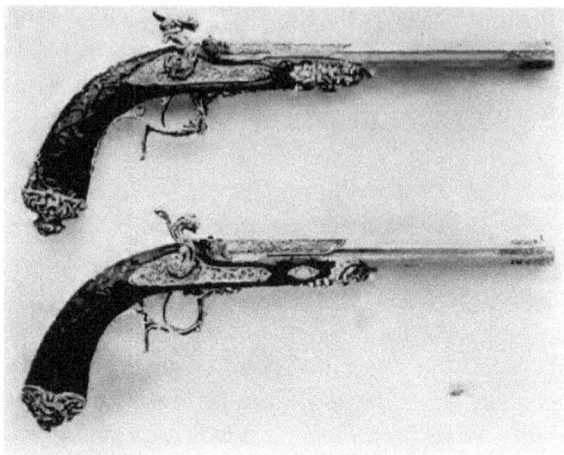

DUELLING PISTOLS BY GASTINNE-RENETTE
The property of the author

THE GASTINNE-RENETTE CHALLENGE TROPHY

quicker and more surely.

Keep your head well up, and look at the head of the figure instead of at the middle of the bull.

This is a rule: if your last shot was low, look higher; if it was high, look lower.

If you are careful to squeeze, instead of jerking, you are almost sure always to hit the figure, the only misses allowable being a graze of the waist to the left, or under the chin to the right.

In order to make "possibles" (twelve shots make a score and not six, as in England, which increases the difficulty enormously) you have to be very careful of your lateral direction; the vertical direction is comparatively unimportant.

The Gastinne-Renette duelling pistol is made in three styles (see picture following page).

The top one shows the breech-loading model; the middle one the muzzle-loading model; and the lowest one the semi-breech-loading model.

This last is intended to combine the accuracy of the muzzle-loader with the ease of loading of the breech-loader.

The powder is poured down the muzzle in the same way that the muzzle-loader is loaded; then the barrel is slid forward by the lever connected with the trigger-guard, the muzzle of the pistol being held vertically in order that the powder may not be spilled.

The powder is now found to be tilling the thimble-like breech. The bullet is placed on the top of this thimble, and the barrel is closed by returning the lever to its place.

Finally a cap is placed on the nipple, and the loading is complete.

Though this of course takes longer than does the loading of a breech-loading pistol, it is easier for an amateur to accomplish than is the loading of a muzzle-loader.

I doubt, however, whether with expert loaders it is as quick as loading a muzzle-loader.

Breaking "plates" (i. e., large saucers) "Au Commandement" is easy; but to break a hundred of them in order to win a gilt medal requires care, also a certain amount of strength and condition.

The gold medal for shooting at sixteen yards with a duelling pistol at the target shown on page 139 is competed for both in deliberate shooting and "Au Commandement." In the former, twelve shots must be in, not touching the five ring; in the latter in the four ring.

In former years the "Au Commandement" was shot for with slow

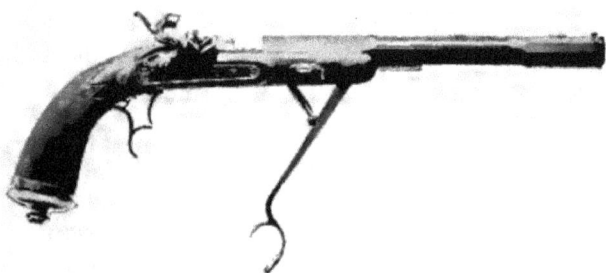

DUELLING PISTOLS
(By Gastinne Renette)

counting, but with the metronome at 100 it is the most difficult of all the medals shot for.

The revolver is also shot a great deal at this gallery; the usual one is the Smith & Wesson, with gallery charge of French powder and a round bullet, either the .44 Russian model or the .38 Army model double action, which is also a Smith & Wesson.

I have described, in my chapters on gallery and stage shooting, how to use the former.

At Gastinne-Renette's there are many medals to be shot for with it, and a gold medal similar to the one for the duelling pistol in deliberate shooting can be shot for; but there is none for rapid firing or for shooting a revolver with double action, which I think is a pity.

The double action .38 calibre is used in the yearly competition at the twenty-five metres man figure, when six shots are fired in twenty seconds, and then a second series of six, constituting a total score of twelve.

It is not permissible to cock the pistol, or yet to raise it, until the word "*feu*" is called.

Two scores of 12 shots each to count (not necessarily consecutive scores.)

It is one or two points easier than the "*Au Commande*ment" with the duelling pistol.

The first shot takes a long time to get off, but twenty-seconds gives plenty of time for the six shots. I generally get mine off in from fifteen to seventeen seconds.

The great thing is to draw back the trigger so as not to jerk off; this is rather tiring to the trigger-finger and cannot be long continued.

Another form of shooting this is to fire at two men figures alternately; in doing so six hits in four seconds have been scored.

CHAPTER 12

Le Pistolet Club

This is a Paris club which holds its meetings at Gastinne-Renette's Gallery for competitions especially with the duelling pistol under duelling conditions, but there are also occasionally competitions with the revolver. The usual competitions consist of:

Shooting "*Au Commande*ment" at the "man" at twenty-five metres, in pairs. Each competitor shoots once against every other competitor, and the greatest number of hits wins. A hit anywhere counts only one point, but half a point is added to the one to shoot first of each pair.

Raising the pistol before the word "*feu*," or shooting after the word "*trois*," counts as a zero even if the target be hit.

There is an elaborate table that indicates which members (the competitors' order of shooting) shoot against each other, and which has the right-hand stand, so that each has an equal chance.

A fee of a *franc* only is charged, and the winner gets a medal.

Another form of shooting is as above, but hits count according to their value, as in ordinary competitions. A third is "*le tir au pigeon*," in which the rule is "first miss out," the one who can keep in longest without a miss, winning.

Sometimes there are competitions at the "running rabbit," or rapid firing at the "man " with revolvers.

This club has among its members the very best pistol-shots in the world, under duelling conditions, men who can get their shots off instantaneously and with extreme accuracy.

Shooting against another man and trying to get your shot off before he does is much more difficult to accomplish than shooting by yourself and merely trying not to be later than "*trois*."

This is a very exclusive club, only men of a certain social standing being admitted.

They never shoot big charges, or use a heavy trigger-pull, though in England, as already stated, this is deemed necessary.

If a man can hold his own in these competitions he may consider himself a first-class shot, and all the shooting is practical, and not target shooting.

The counting is quicker than 100 to the minute.

CHAPTER 13

Competitions With the Devilliers Bullet

Devilliers has patented a bullet for practising duelling, the competitors shooting at each other. The bullet is useful also for in-door shooting where a leaden bullet would be dangerous.

The composition of the bullet is a secret, but the bullet is light, and, when propelled by a cap with fulminate only, gives a hard rap where it strikes. When shooting with it at a man the following precautions must be observed, according to the inventor.

1. "Don't shoot at less than twenty metres." It is useless to shoot with it at more than twenty metres, as the bullet rapidly loses its accuracy beyond that distance; the blow at twenty metres distance is not severe if one is properly protected.

2 . "Wear goggles, a fencing mask, and gloves." The goggles are now made part of the mask, and are of very thick glass, while, instead of the shooter's wearing a glove, a metal shield is affixed to the pistol (see illustration). *The hand must not be lowered before your opponent fires.* I once shot against a friend who omitted this precaution, and my bullet cut away the flesh at the lower part of his thumb.

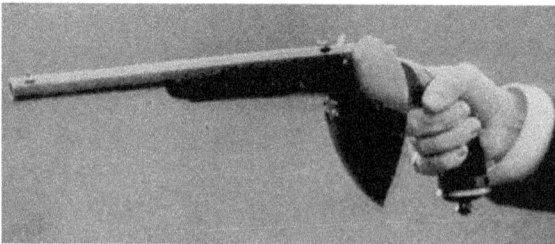

HOW TO HOLD THE DUELLING PISTOL WITH GUARD
FOR SHOOTING DEVILLIER'S BULLET

Position for "Attention"

3. "Wear a black linen blouse." This may be necessary to prevent your clothes being soiled, but it makes you a bigger target for your opponent. Therefore a tight-fitting coat is better. I shoot with no body protection.

4. "In winter be careful that the bullets do not freeze." I find it best to keep the loaded pistols on ice for some time before shooting—not letting them freeze, however—and not to let the pistol get too hot, for if the bullet gets warm it loses its accuracy through not taking the rifling properly.

5. "In summer cool the bullets as much as possible." This I quite agree with.

The bullets are loaded as follows. First you get from the maker some empty cartridge cases, also caps. Then you put the bullet lightly into the mouth of the cartridge, taking care not to press it in or, by squeezing it with your fingers, put it out of shape. Next you insert it into the breech of your pistol—keeping the muzzle up so that the bullet may not drop out owing to its not fitting the cartridge tightly. Finally you lower the muzzle of the pistol and insert the cap, and then close the breech.

When the cartridge has been fired there may be difficulty in extracting the cap for reloading the cartridge. If that be so, push out the cap by inserting a wire into the mouth of the cartridge and pushing inside the cap. But don't attempt to do this with a loaded cap!

The competitions take place like Pistolet Club competitions or like a real duel, and preferably in the open air.

Naturally spectators must not stand behind either of the shooters, and in places where there is not a clear space of about a hundred yards behind each, a white linen sheet hung behind each of them will stop

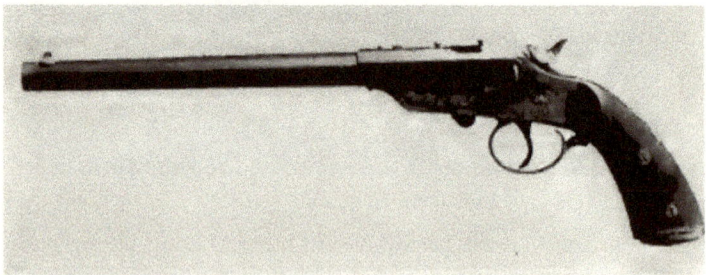

.22 CALIBRE TARGET PISTOL BY LEESON
(Made according to author's specifications)

88

Position when shooting

the bullets. This makes a distinct background, but the effect is better, and the practice too is better, when such sheets are dispensed with.

This kind of shooting makes an amusing game to play at garden parties, *fêtes*, and so on. Also it comes as a novelty after the everlasting round of tennis and croquet parties.

Another form, one very useful for cavalry, is to have a fight on horseback, with revolvers. In such matches the horses' eyes must of course be protected, and a rug and hood should be put on if the animals are nervous or thin-skinned, for a blow at a distance of a few feet would be very severe.

The bullet is also useful for shooting at a paper target, when galloping past. It easily penetrates a playing card and a Bisley target behind it, at five yards.

In fact the invention of this bullet practically solves the problem of how to teach shooting from horseback, if only the barrel of the pistol could be kept cool enough. Perhaps having several pistols and using them alternately is the best way to get over this difficulty.

The bullet is also useful for stage shooting when shooting objects off persons' heads, or out of their hands or mouths, especially if the fingers of the assistant are protected by steel thimbles under his gloves when he holds cards to be shot at, of if a steel skull cap be worn under false hair when the object to be shot at is placed upon his head.

It must be remembered, however, that the bullets are not as accurate as leaden bullets propelled by powder.

Never have any other bullets lying near when shooting Devilliers bullets, as one of the former might be used by mistake and so cause a fatal accident.

THE AUTHOR

CHAPTER 14

Duelling

The mere word duelling appears to shallow minds a subject for so-called "humour," like mothers-in-law and cats, but a moment's thought will show that, in certain circum-stances, the duel forms the only possible solution to a difficulty. And it is not an unmixed blessing that duelling is abolished in England as "Vanoc" in *The Referee* truly says:

> For some reasons, the abolition of duelling [he means in England] is a mistake. Insolent and offensive language is now too frequently indulged in with impunity. . . . The best rule of all is never to take liberties yourself, and never to allow liberties to be taken with you, and to remember that self-defence is still the noble art."

I think, though, that the still nobler art is the defence of others, and there are cases—which need not be gone into here—when a man *must* fight.

One of the reasons for this "humorous" attitude in the English mind (it does not exist abroad) is because sometimes young men, wishing to advertise themselves, or their political ideas, fight duels, all the time never intending to hit each other, and in fact intentionally firing in the air.

When two good shots "mean business," a pistol duel is a very deadly affair, as is shown by the number of men who have been killed in them.

A duel with swords gives more advantage to a younger or a taller man, or to a man in the pink of condition, but a pistol duel will enable a much older man to hold his own.

The challenged has the right to chose weapons, and if he choose

THE POSITION OF SOME DUELLISTS AT THE WORD "ATTENTION"

pistols it is understood that the meeting should be conducted with single-shot duelling pistols.

The British public are accustomed to confuse the words "pistol" and "revolver," and most pistol duels are described as "duels with revolvers" by those not understanding such things; but the revolver is not recognised as a duelling weapon, and any fight with revolvers would on the Continent lead to a trial for murder if anyone were killed.

In challenging, the person considering himself aggrieved asks two of his friends to act as his seconds, and these he sends to his adversary. The latter at once appoints two seconds for himself, and the four seconds then make all the necessary arrangements.

First they call upon a gunmaker—combatants in a duel are not allowed to use their own weapons—and two single-shot muzzle-loading duelling pistols of regulation pattern are chosen.

In the presence of the seconds these are loaded by the gunmaker and put into a case, which is then sealed.

This case is taken to the duelling ground by the gunmaker and the seal is not broken until everything else is ready, the reason of course being to prevent tampering with the pistols, or loads, or obtaining practice with that particular pair of pistols.

A doctor is present at the duel with all necessary appliances.

On the ground the seconds draw lots for where their men are to stand, it being of advantage to have sun and wind at one's back, or left rear.

The distance is twenty-five metres, marked by canes stuck in the ground, and the shooters stand facing each other.

When all is in readiness, the seconds break the seal of the pistol case, then the director of the duel takes the weapons out, holding them by the barrels, one pistol in each hand, and presents the butt ends to the duellist to whom the lot has fallen to have first choice. The other pistol is handed to his adversary.

If shots are exchanged without result, the duellists exchange places for the next shot.

It is not permissible to try the trigger-pull by cocking and lowering the hammer, but about how light or heavy the pull is can be ascertained to some extent when cocking. A light click indicates a light pull, and a loud click a heavier one.

It is usual, especially if the duellists are good shots, and if they happen to be very angry with each other, to give them a very heavy

THE AUTHOR'S POSITION AT "ATTENTION"

trigger-pull in order to make it more difficult for them to hit each other. Therefore it is well always to give a good strong pull back when firing, so as to avoid pulling off to the side if you have been given a very heavy trigger-pull.

For the same reason the words of command in such cases are given very quickly. This prevents getting aim.

Finally the duellists cock their pistols, the seconds stand clear, and the director of the fight stands midway between the duellists and about six metres back of the line between them.

The duellists stand with their right elbows touching their right hips, butt of pistol to thigh, and their pistols pointing at the ground.

The director calls: "Attention—*Feu! Un—deux—trois!*"

If either is not ready at the word "attention," he says so, but otherwise *after* the word "*feu*" he raises his pistol and must fire before the word "*trois*" is spoken.

If he does not have his elbow to his hip, and muzzle to ground; or if he raises his pistol or even moves it before the word "*feu*"; or if he fires after the word "*trois*" has been spoken, and he kills his man, he is liable, if his adversary's seconds lodge a complaint, to be tried for murder.

The usual speed at which these words are spoken is a hundred words to the minute, but, as I have said, the director often hurries the words in order to baffle the duellists and prevent their injuring each other fatally.

Whether the duel should continue if neither combatant is sufficiently injured after the interchange of shots to prevent his going on shooting is a matter that the seconds have arranged between them before the duel begins. It depends chiefly upon the gravity of the reason for which the duel is fought.

The position to stand in, in my opinion, should not be quite sideways.

Of course one should, theoretically, make as small a target as possible for one's opponent, and therefore the coat should be buttoned close. But whereas if standing quite sideways one makes a smaller mark, if hit when in that position the wound will probably prove more dangerous.

A bullet which would perforate both lungs of a man standing sideways, will most likely go through one lung only if he be standing more full face. Several other internal organs are also safer when the shooters stand full face; by leaning forward the ribs are closer together and afford protection to the heart and lungs, also from a shooting

CORRECT POSITION AT THE MOMENT OF FIRING

point of view, one can make much better practice when standing more or less facing the object to be hit, than when craning one's head round to try and look over one's right shoulder, and so hampering one's right arm.

It is generally considered that one should look as dark as possible to one's opponent, and turn up one's collar to avoid showing a white mark. But with this I am not sure that I quite agree. Personally I should prefer to shoot at an entirely black target without a white collar or white patch anywhere diverting one's eye, unless that white was at a place one wanted to hit.

For instance, if a very bad shot were going to fire at me, I should prefer his trying to hit my collar, as he would then be more likely to shoot over my head, or to miss me by shooting past me, than if he tried to hit me in the middle of the body.

The white collar would, however, be hidden by the right hand and pistol as soon as the pistol was raised, if aim were taken at an opponent's head.

The position safest *for yourself* is to aim at your opponent's head, and to get on to that position immediately after the word "*feu*," keeping your own head low.

Your right hand and the pistol-butt protect your throat and a good deal of your face and head if you lower your face as much as possible.

Some men stand in the position of lunging in fencing, which makes a still smaller target of the body, but then this exposes them to a more raking fire, and a shot which would only pierce the thigh of the right leg, if the duellist were standing upright, might glance along the thigh and penetrate the abdomen if he were standing in a lunging attitude.

A level-headed man, however, would never agree to fight a duel unless he deemed it justifiable, and then most likely his whole attention would be concentrated upon killing his opponent, and considerations, of personal safety would be neglected; in the same way that a steeple-chase rider thinks only of winning and not of his personal safety—if it is otherwise he is no good as a cross-country rider.

As the great object is to hit an opponent before he hits you,—as, if he hits you first, even slightly, he may spoil your aim,—it is better to hit him as low as possible, provided the bullet strikes high enough to injure him.

It takes time to raise the pistol to the level of his head, or even of his armpit, whereas with practice you can flip the wrist up and hit him

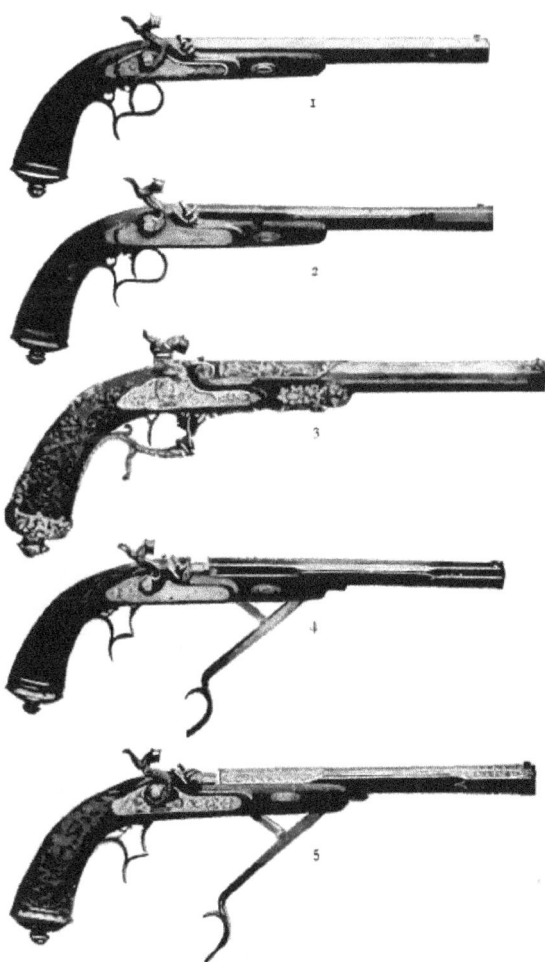

PISTOLS BY GASTINNE RENETTE
1. Muzzle-loading duelling pistol.
2. Muzzle-loading duelling pistol of higher finish.
3. Chased muzzle-loading duelling pistol.
4. Sliding-action duelling pistol.
5. Higher-finished sliding-action duelling pistol

in the thigh or hip without raising the arm at all, and almost before the word "*Un.*"

If you hit him in the thigh it would not be of much use in a serious duel, so the hip level is the point to try for.

An instance of perfect timing was that of a recent fatal duel where one man killed the other immediately after "*feu*," before his adversary had time to raise his pistol.

In the report of a certain duel which took place in France recently, several of the English papers made humorous reference to one of the duellists not firing his pistol (he placed it behind his back) at the word "*feu*." The writers seemed to think he had forgotten to fire, because, when questioned as to his conduct, he said, "*J'ai oublie.*" Of course anyone conversant with duelling must have known that by acting thus he meant that he did not desire to kill or to wound his adversary. A good shot who for any reason did not wish to hit his adversary would always put his pistol behind him rather than shoot wide and get credit for making a miss. It is more dignified to do this, if one does not want to shoot an adversary, than to miss on purpose. Moreover, the latter act might be misconstrued into an attempt to kill.

By French law, if a man is killed in a duel, the body must be left where it fell, the police informed at once. The police then make an investigation. The adversary is arrested and tried subsequently at the Court of Assizes. He ought, of course, to stop by the body and give him-self up. He and his seconds may be condemned to imprisonment.

Not wanting to kill an adversary is also the reason so many duels are bloodless. Men, in the heat of an argument, challenge each other. In cooler moments, they see that the cause of quarrel was not of sufficient importance to warrant their killing, or attempting to kill each other. Yet neither likes to apologise lest this should look like cowardice; so the two exchange a shot, and both miss on purpose.

In this connection I may mention that the American law does not apply in the case of a duel fought by a citizen of the United States outside the geographical limits of that country; for, according to Mr. R. Newton Crane, no offence is committed by the fact that an American citizen has participated in a duel beyond the jurisdiction of the United States. The citizenship of the combatant is, in such circumstances, immaterial.

"On the other hand sending, knowingly bearing, or accepting a challenge, in England or America, renders the sender, bearer, or accepter liable to punishment by the laws of England or America as the case may be, whether the duel is subsequently fought or not, and whether it is fought in England or America or abroad, and whether the offending party is an Englishman, American, or a foreigner. Provoking a man to send a challenge is also an indictable offence.

The law applicable to the punishment for actually fighting the duel is, on the other hand, the law of the place where the duel is fought, and that law only applies to the offence.

Provocation, however great, is no excuse, though it might weigh with the court in fixing the punishment. Under the English law the punishment for sending, bearing, or accepting a challenge is fine or imprisonment without hard labour, or both. Each of the States of the United States has penalties for the offence, which though differing in detail are practically the same in substance as those provided by the English law."

CHAPTER 15

The .22 Calibre Single-Shot Pistol

The .22 calibre long-barrelled single-shot pistol is used for target and small game shooting.

There are several American and Continental makes of the .22 calibre single-shot pistol. I give illustrations of some of them, but they are all more or less similar. In the United States these pistols are used for target shooting up to fifty yards, also for taking out on shooting trips where the rifle is used for big game, and the .22 pistol for shooting small game for food where a shotgun would alarm more important game.

On the Continent it is little used, but the Olympic Games fifty-yards pistol championship led to a certain amount of practice with it, as it is the weapon for that range.

Up to sixteen metres I consider the .4 calibre duel-ling pistol (muzzle-loader) the most accurate of all pistols for stationary target shooting, as the slightly greater accuracy possessed by the .22 calibre, shooting long rifle ammunition, is more than counterbalanced by the larger hole cut by the duelling pistol, a .22 bullet often missing the bull, whereas the larger ball cuts into it.

From twenty yards upward the .22 beats both the duelling pistol and the revolver in the order named; at fifty yards the .22 comes first, the revolver is a bad second, and the duelling pistol is nowhere.

The .22 is often made with a rear sight capable of elevation and of lateral movement by a screw adjustment. It is always made with a very light trigger-pull.

The trigger is very close to the grip so that one has to pull with the second or even with the third joint of the trigger-finger.

This is, in my opinion, a very grave fault. I have not found any pistol of this calibre with the trigger sufficiently far forward to suit me,

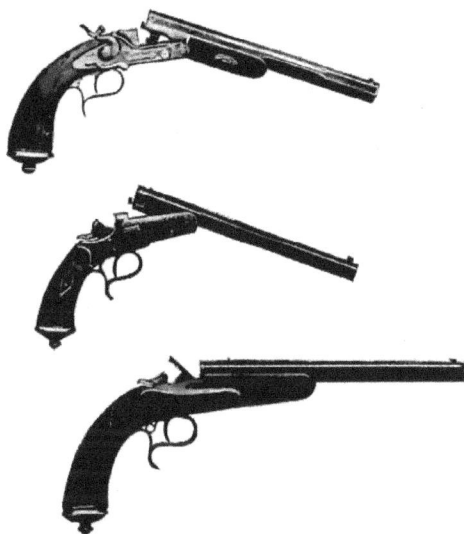

PISTOLS BY GASTINNE-RENETTE

1. Shooting Smith & Wesson, .44 cartridge.
2. Modified Ira Paine to shoot .44 or .22 ammunition.
3. Saloon pistol, .22 bore, weighing and balancing like
   a duelling pistol

STEVENS DIAMOND MODEL PISTOL
6-inch barrel; weight, S 3-4 oz.; .22 cal.

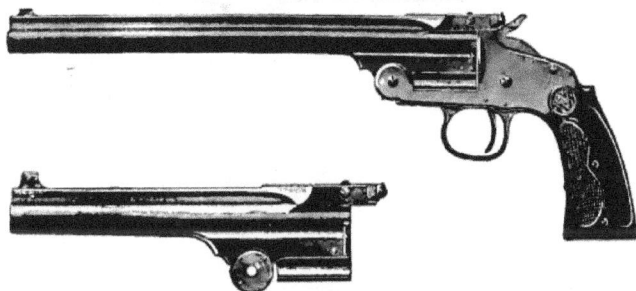

.22 SMITH & WESSON PISTOL WITH INTERCHANGEABLE
.32 BARREL

WURFFLEIN PISTOL
10-inch barrel; weight, 2 lbs. 2 oz.; .22 cal.

SMITH & WESSON PISTOL
10-inch barrel; weight 1 lb. 8 3-4 oz.; .22 cal.

STEVENS PISTOL, GOULD MODEL
10-inch barrel; weight 1 lb. 12 oz.; .22 cal.

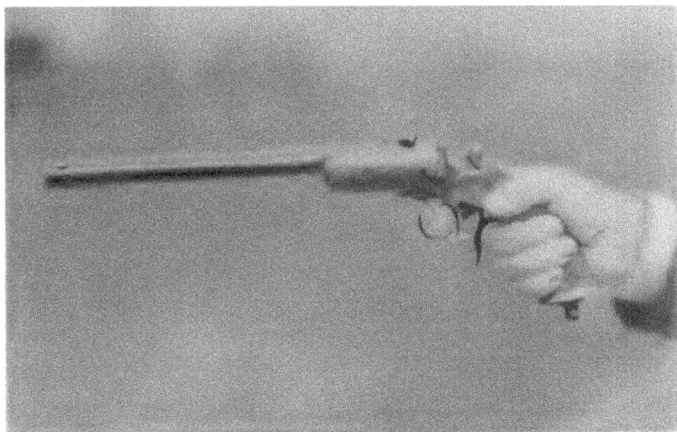

How to hold the Gastinne-Renette modification of the Stevens, showing trigger well forward

Stevens Off-Hand Target

STEVENS "LORD"

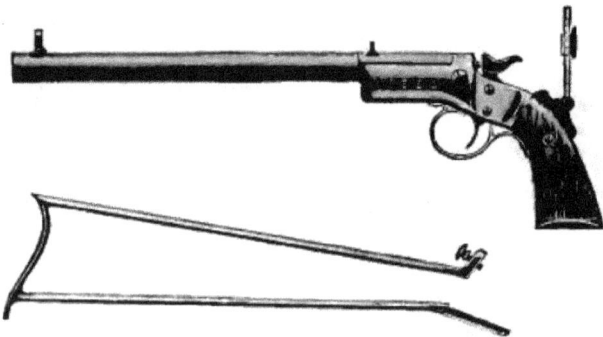

STEVENS VERNIER NEW MODEL POCKET "RIFLE"

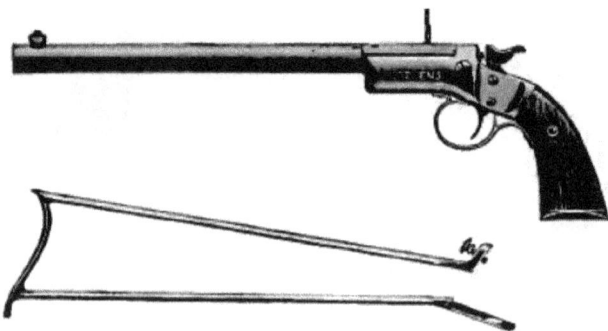

STEVENS NEW MODEL POCKET OR BICYCLE "RIFLE"

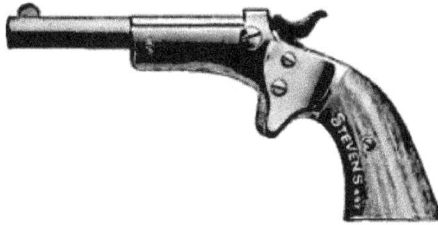

STEVENS "TIP-UP"

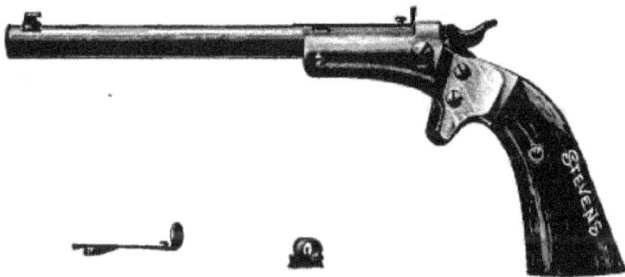

Peep Rear   Globe Front

STEVENS "DIAMOND"

FIG. 1   FIG. 2   FIG. 3

WEBLEY MAN-STOPPING BULLET

Fig. 1 Bullet & case being fired.

Fig. 2 Bullet after it has entered the flesh.

Fig. 3 Section of bullet after explosion.

POLICE TARGET DOUBLE-ACTION COLT REVOLVER

but I do not take enough interest in a .22 pistol to have one specially made.

It is only a toy, and except for a special competition, such as the one at the Olympic Games, it is not worth practising with. For ladies, however, it is well suited on account of its small cartridge.

CHAPTER 15

Team Shooting and Coaching

When you are a member of a team, do exactly what the captain of the team directs you to do. Never mind if you think that he is wrong, and that you could do better work in your own way. It is "his show," and he alone is responsible; merely shoot as well as you can in his way. Of course, if he should ask your advice, that is a different thing. Should another member of your team ask advice, refer him to the captain.

If you are captain of a team, and have the choice of men, select, preferably, men whose nerve can be relied upon; a veteran who does not get "rattled," even if only a moderate shot, is preferable to a brilliant beginner who may go all to pieces at a critical moment.

The man I prefer in a team is one who always shoots a good consistent score,—never brilliantly, yet never badly; you can always rely upon him to shoot up to his form. If you have two such men, let one of them shoot the first score,—if possible, against your adversaries' best man,—so as to give your team confidence that they are likely to hold their own.

Reserve yourself—or your most reliable shot, who can be trusted not to lose his head—for emergencies, such as these: To shoot last, when everything depends upon making a good score; when the light is bad and likely to improve later; if there is a wind that may drop later; for pulling up a score when the other team is leading; for getting the sighting when you retire to the fifty-yards range; to shoot "turn and turn about," against the most nervous or dangerous man of the other team, and so on.

You should specially notice if any of your team are getting nervous; prevent their watching good shooting by their adversaries, or looking at and comparing scores. Encourage them to think that their own team is so strong that their own individual shortcomings do not

matter. You can, in this way, "nurse" a man along who is on the verge of "going to pieces."

If possible, do not let your men know how the scores stand. If there is a wind, or rain or bad light, consult your most "weather-wise" man, and decide how to "place" your bad shots so as to give them the easiest "shoot." That is to say, if the wind is likely to drop later, shoot your strong shots when the weather is unfavourable.

It is also a good thing to have a reliable member of the team stand behind each one who is shooting, to "spot" for him, and keep time for him.

If there be a time limit, have a very good man, if possible, at the left elbow of each shooter, with a stop watch. His business, if the time limit is, let us say, three minutes for the six shots, to start his watch when the signal to begin firing is given; to say "one minute" at the end of the first minute; "two minutes" at the end of the second minute; and then, "fifteen," "thirty," and "forty-five," at the ends of the first three quarters respectively of the last minute, and finally to count "one," "two," "three," etc., for the last fifteen seconds.

This lets the shooter know *exactly* how much time he has, and enables him to make the utmost use of lulls of wind.

Also at each shot he must say, "bull," if the shot is well in the bull, or "inch out seven" if under the bull to the left, etc., thus enabling the shooter to correct his aim for the next shot.

It is quite wrong to say the *value* of the shot. What the shooter wants to know is how to correct his next shot, if the previous one was wrong; the value of a shot does not help him to know where he ought to aim.

For this reason a "coach" who is not properly drilled is much worse than useless. He is a hindrance and confuses the shooter. For instance, if he says, "Oh, only a five," that conveys no meaning to the shooter as to where his shot has gone, and he has to ask, "Is it high or low?" The coach answers, "It's a long way off the bull; how did you come to make such a bad shot? It is to the right." Probably the shooter then asks, "Is it low?" and the coach answers, "Yes—no—it isn't. It's right on top," and so on, to the exasperation of the shooter and the spoiling of the score. Shooter and coach should practise together, so that their minds work together, and instantaneously. Only the actual spot struck should be told, and that instantly, and in the fewest possible words.

"Oh's," and all such exclamations, ought to be rigorously avoided. Coaching is allowed in team shooting, *but not in ordinary individual*

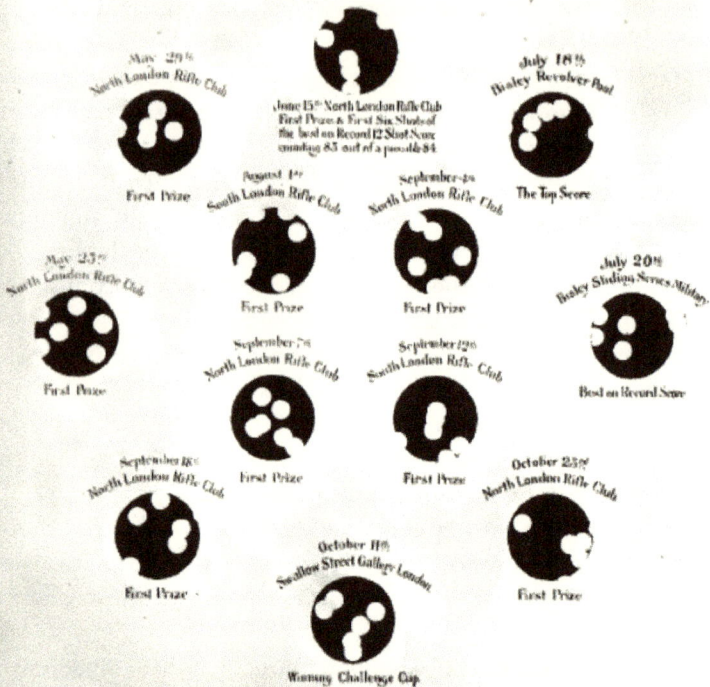

DIAGRAMS OF TWELVE HIGHEST POSSIBLE SCORES MADE BY AUTHOR IN
REVOLVER COMPETITIONS AT 20 YARDS IN 1895
The diameter of the original bull's-eyes is 2 inches

competitions.

Do not let any member of your team leave the range on any account until the competition is over.

Have a man or two extra, in case of anything disabling or preventing one of your team from shooting.

Do not let two men shoot with the same revolver, as both men may be wanted to shoot at the same time.

Do not scold a man, however badly he may be doing; you only flurry him, and it does no good.

Do not have any refreshments for your team until the competition is over.

CHAPTER 16

General Remarks on Shooting in Competitions

When shooting in competition, be careful not to spoil your opponent's scores. Never approach or leave the firing-point while he is aiming or about to shoot. If he is about to shoot, and there be time, reserve your shot till he has fired; and do not fidget with your revolver or cartridges or get your target drawn up whilst he is aiming. Keep perfectly still and silent till his shot has gone off. Do not speak to him at any time, except to answer some question of his. If he is at all nervous, you might by a slight movement or word ruin his score.

Read carefully, *before* shooting, the rules of the competition in which you are about to engage, and be sure you comply with every detail of them. If you find you have, inadvertently, transgressed a rule, report to the range officer at once, and get your score cancelled.

Write your name very distinctly on your scorecard; I have known a man to lose a prize owing to his name being illegible on the scorecard. See that your shots have been entered properly and rightly added up and the corrections initialled.

Have your target dated and signed by the range officer, with the name of the competition also inscribed, and keep it as evidence in case your card should get lost. Be sure you do not by mistake have a score entered on a ticket belonging to another series.

Before shooting at Bisley, I put a weight in a chemist's scale equal to the average weight of one of my loaded cartridges. I weigh each cartridge against it, put all of the correct weight aside for Bisley, and keep the others for practice. By this means I minimise the chance of a weak or of too strong a shot.

When you are at the firing-point, pay no attention to what anyone else is doing, or to what scores have been, or are being, made, or to any of your scores being beaten; the great thing is to have the average all round high for the aggregate prizes. If you are constantly watching the scores of others, rushing from range to range as your various scores are passed, you will have much less chance of making good scores than if you keep plodding on, constantly adding a point or two to your aggregate. You can afterwards try to beat individual scores, if necessary. Of course, if you at any time, in any one series, get a score which you think is up to the limit of your skill, you may let that series alone till you have reached your limit in all other series. Never watch a good man shooting; it will only make you doubt if you can beat him. It is also tiring your eyes uselessly.

Do not read or use your eyes any more than is absolutely necessary. When resting, dark glasses will be found to relieve the eyes. I find that if I am getting tired of shooting, a half-hour's gallop on a horse that does not pull freshens me up, and helps to divert my thoughts; others may prefer lying quietly down and shutting the eyes.

If you find yourself getting stale, drop the whole thing, even for several days. It will not be time wasted, as you will shoot better afterwards; and you will certainly get worse if you keep on without rest.

Never protest or dispute a score or a decision. The range officers are doing their best under very trying circumstances. If you think any decision wrong, say nothing about it and forget it; you will only spoil your shooting if you worry about it. Just set your teeth and make a score a point better than the disputed one ought, in your opinion, to have been. The protesting man is a nuisance to himself and to everyone else.

Should you see a man infringing the rules, leave it to others to protest.

CHAPTER 17

Automatic Pistols

There have been various automatic pistols made which load and cock by the force of the discharge of the previous shot. The one with which I can shoot best is the Webley-Fosbery Automatic Revolver here illustrated.

The recoil causes the upper part of the revolver to fly back, a stud acting in a zigzag groove in the chamber half turning the chamber as it flies back, and completing the revolution as it returns to its normal position by the force of a spring which has been compressed by the discharge.

I can shoot very well with this, but I cannot try it against the double-action .38 Smith & Wesson—with which I made the record score of six shots in a two-inch circle at twenty-five metres in seventeen seconds—as it will not shoot gallery ammunition, there not being recoil enough in that to operate the mechanism.

One made specially with a weaker spring for gallery ammunition would be an ideal weapon for rapid firing at Gastinne-Renette's.

Another form of automatic is the Browning, but this is not a target pistol and I cannot make good shooting with it. In my opinion having to use both hands to cock it for the first shot constitutes a defect. One ought to be able to draw, cock, and fire with one hand any pistol intended for self-defence.

Most nations have an automatic pistol of one make or another as their regulation army weapon, but France and the United States keep to the double-action revolver, and they are not the worst pistol shots and they know what a good pistol ought to be.

Personally I should never carry an automatic pistol for self-defence, for use on dangerous game, or for target shooting, as the revolver is so much more handy, shoots better, and it is safer after one shot has

WEBLEY-FOSBERY AUTOMATIC REVOLVER

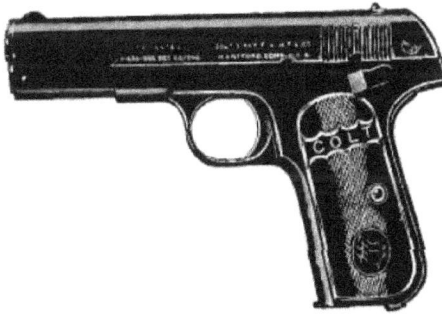

COLT AUTOMATIC PISTOL, POCKET MODEL,
CALIBRE .32

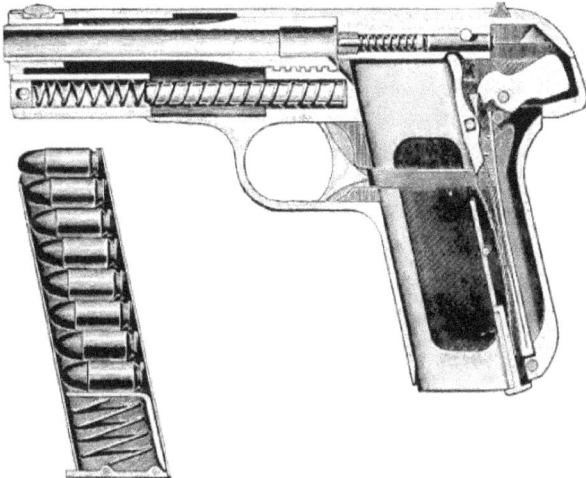

COLT AUTOMATIC PISTOL, CALIBRE .32
Sectional view showing the automatic action

been fired.

I have never seen any score made by any automatic pistol (except the Fosbery, which is really an improved revolver rather than a typical automatic pistol) which was any good.

One ought to be able to take a pistol out of its holster or the pocket, aim, then change one's mind and return it to the pocket, all with one hand.

A double-action revolver you take out, half raise the hammer with the trigger-pull as you level it, decide not to shoot, release the pull, and drop the pistol in your pocket, and it is safe.

With an automatic pistol you draw it, and have to take hold of it with both hands so as to draw the bolt to cock it; when you aim and decide not to shoot you have again to manipulate it with both hands, and in some instances to extract all the cartridges and put them again in the magazine before it is safe to put in the pocket. If you want to return it safely to your pocket after you have fired a shot, the process to be gone through is yet more complicated.

Of course if you blaze away all your cartridges it is quicker than any revolver, but I am talking of the much more frequent occurrence of firing only one or two shots, or of not shooting at all after having drawn the weapon on the chance of needing it, then finding there was no necessity to shoot.

For a lady's use as a weapon of defence I should not for a moment advise an automatic pistol.

In selecting an automatic pistol, as distinct from an automatic re-volver, care must be taken that it has an efficient safety bolt.

As the action for cocking the automatic pistol consists in drawing back the barrel, *if the pistol is dropped so that the barrel strikes the ground with its muzzle* the pistol is very apt to be discharged.

I have heard of such a case which led to fatal results. This seems to me one of the weak points of such pistols, as, even if the pistol has an efficient safety bolt, such a bolt is almost sure to have been moved when the pistol is held in the hand ready to fire, and in such a case, if the pistol is dropped, it will most likely explode. This fact must be borne in mind when choosing between a revolver and an automatic pistol intended for self-defence.

COLT AUTOMATIC PISTOL,
MILITARY MODEL, CALIBRE .45

COLT AUTOMATIC PISTOL,
MILITARY MODEL, CALIBRE .38

LUGAR AUTOMATIC PISTOL

CHAPTER 18

The Revolver in War

Unfortunately war, and not target shooting, is the chief use for revolvers up to the present time, (1911).

As I am not a military man I cannot go as fully into details as I have done with regard to some of the other uses of the revolver; but I should say, speaking as a civilian, that the nearer the revolver approaches to that recommended for big-game shooting (whilst fulfilling the necessary military requirements and regulations), the more useful and re-liable will it be found.

My hints as to shooting deer, or at targets, from horseback, would apply to chasing drivers of retreating guns, or infantry; and my various suggestions for practising rapid firing at moving objects would also apply. The episode of the officers in the Boer War repeatedly missing store bullocks with their revolvers illustrates the need of practice with this arm, which not even an acquaintance with the rifle (supposing the officers to have such) enables one to dispense with.

It is useless to describe in detail the various patterns of automatic pistols and revolvers used by the different nations, as these not only constantly change, so that any I now write about may be obsolete by the time this book is published, but each nation has also its special needs, so that the pistol suitable for one country might not be the best for another.

For instance, in England there seems to be a greater demand than in any other country for a pistol with "stopping power." In consequence, various more or less blunt-nosed bullets have been invented, some of them almost cylinders with cupped tops. Very good shooting is said to have been made with some of these shapes of bullets: personally, though it may be only fancy, I do not think bullets of such shape can fly quite as accurately as those which are pointed, although I have

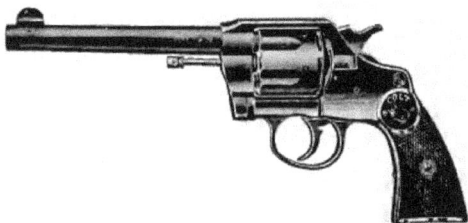

NEW ARMY COLT DOUBLE-ACTION REVOLVER
Adopted by Ordnance Department U. S. Army

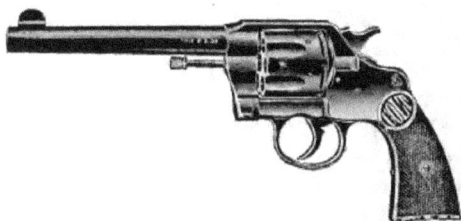

NEW NAVY COLT DOUBLE-ACTION REVOLVER
Adopted by Bureau of Ordnance, U. S. Navy

NEW SERVICE COLT DOUBLE-ACTION REVOLVER
Jointless solid frame, simultaneous ejection

RUSSIAN MODEL ARMY REVOLVER
(Smith & Wesson)

SHOOTING ON HORSEBACK—PURSUING SHOT

done good shooting at deer with them at very short range. I myself have never been able, in experimenting, to improve on the conical shape for extreme accuracy, the spitzen form of bullet being more suitable for arms of higher velocity than for pistols.

The consensus of opinion, however, in all other armies seems now to be in favour of very small calibres, as the advantages of a small calibre over a large one in port-ability, lightness, and amount of am-munition that can be carried, are so great that they are considered to outweigh the want of stopping power. A man who cannot hit another in a vital spot at the short range at which a revolver is used in war would not do any better with the larger calibre.

I do not think that the advantages of a pistol over a sword, or even a lance, for cavalry are sufficiently appreciated. Going on the standard of the "Can't-hit-a-haystack " shooting of the ordinary trooper with a revolver, it is not realised what a squadron of cavalry, which could "shoot," might be able to accomplish with this weapon. In charging, which I suppose would very seldom occur in modern warfare, each man could fire several shots at opposing cavalry; whilst their adversar-ies, if cavalry, with only lance and sword, could not have a "go" at them until they got within a yard or two. A lancer, and, in a lesser degree, a trooper, armed with a sword, needs elbow room to wield his weapon; when hemmed in by companions pressing close in on him he cannot use it. An adversary can, moreover, parry, or even clutch, the lance, and then he is quite helpless.

A trooper who was through the Zulu campaign told me that many of the men in his troop threw away their lances and depended on their revolvers in a charge, as Zulus dodged their lances and seized their horses, whereas a revolver cleared the way in charging.

In hand-to-hand cavalry fighting the man with the revolver would have the lancer or swordsman absolutely at his mercy; while as for pursuing, the little bugler-boy in South Africa showed what can be done with a revolver. From the standpoint of the pursued, a man with a lance is helpless, and a swordsman is almost as helpless; but a man with a pistol can keep loading and shooting back at his pursuers all the time he is galloping away at top speed.

An infantry soldier, if active, cool, and a good hand with the bayo-net, especially if he also understands the dislikes and fears of horses, can defend himself against a mounted swordsman or lancer; by prick-ing the horse on the nose, for instance, he can prevent the rider being able to get his horse up close to him; he also can parry a swordcut

SHOOTING ON HORSEBACK—RETIRING SHOT

or lance-thrust, or dodge the blow. But a mounted man with a pistol could shoot at him as he gallops past out of range of his bayonet-lunge, or even stand still on his horse at thirty or forty yards off and shoot him.

I believe that the cavalry on both sides in the United States Civil War made more use of their revolvers than of sword or lance, and the revolvers routed the lances.

A pistol needs much less physical strength to use than either sword or lance, and is no more difficult to learn to handle. Lances, besides, are conspicuous when cavalry-are trying to conceal themselves, and are useless among trees.

Artillery drivers are especially helpless when pursued, yet if properly taught they could use a pistol whilst driving their horses, and prevent the incident I have depicted below, which is founded on fact, though I have, for reasons that are obvious, used fancy uniforms.

Cavalry could be trained with the Devilliers bullet.

CHAPTER 19

Target Shooting off Horseback

When shooting off a standing horse at a stationary mark, turn the horse facing to the left at an angle of forty-five degrees. This is to prevent his flinching at the shots, as any but a very seasoned horse would be sure to do if you shot straight over his head or close past his ears. Also if he were to toss his head when you were shooting over it you might both kill him and get either a rearing backward fall, with the horse on top of you, or else a "purler" over his head. If the horse shies away from the outstretched arm, tie a handkerchief over his off eye, as the bullfighters do, and stuff cotton wool in his ears, until he is accustomed to the noise and flash.

There should be a bar in front of the horse to prevent his getting closer to the target than the distance for which the match is arranged; but if the bar be low, and the horse a good fencer, he is apt to jump at the bar. It is very difficult to get a horse to keep absolutely still, and for that reason it is often more difficult to shoot when the horse is fidgeting than when he is swinging along at a gallop.

For shooting at a gallop or a canter, children's balloons, put up on the "heads and posts" principle, are very good marks as they can be shot at with Devilliers bullets, shooting alternately to the right and left. I can also recommend a target on the principle of the Bisley "running deer," travelling on rails parallel to a railing, on the other side of which the shooter gallops and which prevents his getting too close to the target.

Firing blank ammunition at "lightning paper" stuck in the cleft of a stick is very good practice, is less troublesome than using the Devilliers bullet, which does not stand rapid firing in a hot revolver, and is, moreover, less dangerous to spectators. The paper flares up on being touched by burning particles of powder, but of course the shooting

Shooting off horseback charging

must be done at a distance of a few feet only.

I do not think there is much advantage in cantering too slowly; the speed at which the horse goes smoothest, without raking or boring, is the best.

For practical purposes, shooting behind one when galloping is useful. It is an assistance, when first learning, to catch hold of the pommel of the saddle with the bridle hand as you swing your body round to fire. When shooting alternately to right and left, be sure to lift the muzzle of the revolver clear of the horse's head as you swing it from side to side, or you may shoot your horse in the head if he should happen to toss it at that moment.

With modern, high-velocity, nickel-jacketed rifle-bullets it is useless to try sheltering yourself behind the body of your horse, when being shot at with a rifle; but against a revolver-bullet it may be useful. To do this, catch hold of the horse's mane with the bridle hand, sink your body down along his neck on the side farthest from your adversary, hook your left heel against the cantle of your saddle, and shoot at him under your horse's neck as you come quartering diagonally towards him. A tall man on a small horse can get very well round the horse's neck. As you pass, you can take a parting shot diagonally behind you under your left arm past your horse's quarters without shifting your position.

There is a lot of sport and practice to be got out of shooting at each other in pairs with the Devilliers bullet, having, besides the usual protection for the shooters, the horses protected with horse clothing and their eyes with thick glass. The shooting is done either by charging past each other or circling round each other, spectators keeping out of range.

CHAPTER 20

Shooting in Self-Defence

This chapter is written entirely from the technical point of view as a branch of revolver shooting, while the legal aspect of the question is treated by law experts in the Appendix. Whether there is justification, in self-defence, in killing anyone is another matter, but of course cases occur when a man must shoot in order to save someone dependent upon him. Fortunately in the great majority of cases the object of protecting oneself—or, what is more important, protecting someone else—is attained without actually shooting. The mere fact of being armed is generally sufficient, and in many cases wearing the revolver openly or having it in one's hand, even unloaded, suffices. As Polonius says: "*Beware of entrance to a quarrel, but being in, bear 't that the opposed one may beware of thee.*" But, if shooting *has* to be done, everything depends on *getting the first shot*.

As I said above, I am *not* dealing with the ethical aspect of the case; and, putting *that* aside, if you can take your adversary unawares, and "get the drop on him" before he gets it on you, you have him at your mercy.

A short-barrelled revolver is best if it has to be concealed, but of as big a calibre as you can carry without its being too bulky and showing in your pocket. If there be no necessity for concealment, carry one six inches in the barrel.

Some prefer a large-bore army revolver, with the barrel cut down to two inches. I am assuming that the shooting will be done at a distance of only a few feet, and without aim in the ordinary sense of the word.

As elsewhere explained, it is very dangerous to carry an ordinary revolver loaded in the pocket, even at half-cock, especially if it be a self-cocker.

SMITH & WESSON HAMMERLESS SAFETY REVOLVERS
.38 AND .32 CALIBRE

MECHANISM OF THE SMITH & WESSON
HAMMERLESS SAFETY REVOLVER
A, Safety Lever; B, Safety Catch; C, Hammer;
D, Trigger; G, Safety Latch Spring

The proper way with a single-action revolver is to leave one chamber unloaded and to lower the hammer on that empty chamber.

The Smith & Wesson .38 calibre safety hammerless pocket revolver obviates these risks. This revolver cannot go off accidentally, even when all the chambers are loaded, as there is a safety catch which prevents the revolver from being discharged unless it is pressed at the same time that the trigger is pulled.

Anyone used to revolver shooting, who holds it as I have described in my instructions for revolver shooting, and *squeezes the trigger,* will be able to shoot without thinking of the safety catch, for he presses it unconsciously in gripping the stock. A person not accustomed to a revolver cannot, however, fire it; in fact, if a man not an expert revolver-shot wrested the revolver from you, it would be harmless in his hands against you. Indeed, the pistol could without danger be given, loaded, to a small child to play with, as it requires a stronger grip than a child's to discharge it.

Most revolver accidents occur through the hammer receiving an accidental blow, slipping from the thumb or catching in something, or from the trigger being touched unintentionally, or the revolver being left at full-cock.

In the Smith & Wesson safety revolver all these causes of accident are impossible, and it is always ready for instant use. Its further advantages are:

1. There is no external hammer to catch in anything.

2. Pressure on the trigger cannot discharge the revolver unless the stock is properly grasped at the same time.

3. The revolver cannot be kept at full-cock.

4. Being hammerless, and having no projections, it can be drawn more quickly than an ordinary revolver.

5. It can be carried with absolute safety loaded in the pocket, with the knowledge that a fall or blow will not discharge it.

This revolver is also made in smaller calibre (.32), with both 3 in. and 1½ in. barrel. In the latter case it is called a bicycle revolver, and takes up less room in the pocket.

This calibre might be better for a lady's use; but for a man I prefer the larger calibre, as being more powerful. A .44 calibre made on this model would be best of all for a man to carry.

The cocking by trigger action in this revolver is so arranged that it

SELF-DEFENCE—AT BAY

can, with a little practice, be held at full-cock whilst the aim is taken, instead of the cocking and firing being a continuous action, as in other double-action revolvers.

Carrying the revolver in the hip pocket is in my opinion a mistake, as the movement of putting back the hand to draw will instantly put an adversary on his guard and most likely draw his fire.

For a case where you are likely to be robbed, the inside breast-pocket (where banknotes are usually carried) is a good place for the revolver, as, when you are asked for your money, you can appear to be taking it out of this pocket whilst you are really drawing the revolver; or the revolver can be shot from this pocket without drawing it.

Usually the right-hand side-pocket of a jacket is the handiest, or, rather, the pocket on the side of the hand you can shoot with best.

Shooting through the pocket is as quick and unexpected a way as any; another is to turn partly away, and in doing so draw and fire from behind your back, or under your other arm.

But, assuming that you would prefer, if possible, to capture your assailant without shooting him, try whether you cannot unexpected "get the drop" (*i.e.*, an aim) on him and make him hold up his hands before he can draw his revolver

As in fencing and boxing, the great thing is never to take your eyes off your opponent for an instant; and if by any subterfuge you can induce him to take his eyes off you, or distract his attention to anything else, then is the time to "get the drop" on him, or, as a last resource, to shoot.

Knocking a chair over, throwing something past or at him with your non-shooting hand, or calling out to some imaginary, or real, person behind him may often have the desired effect.

If he is a really "bad" man, and armed, the worst thing you can do is to take a revolver in your hand—or even make towards it—unless you mean to shoot instantly; it will only draw his fire, or he may un-expectedly disarm you in the way described below.

Supposing you are unarmed and your adversary has a revolver, you may be able to render his weapon harmless by ejecting his cartridges.

The way to do this varies with different makes of revolvers, but the principle in each case with a revolver having a "breakdown" action consists in making a downward stroke on the barrel of his revolver with one of your hands, and in the same movement operating the opening catch or lever with your thumb.

If you get an assistant to take an empty revolver and point it at you, and you practise this trick, you will find it very simple and effective; but of course there would be no use in trying it with an adversary who suspected you were about to do so. The Smith & Wesson Russian Model can be rendered harmless by seizing the middle of the barrel with your thumb under the catch, you being to the left and using your right hand, or *vice versa*. Simultaneously with seizing the revolver give a quick quarter turn to your wrist to the right, and all the cartridges will fly out.

With the Webley, you place your thumb *over* instead of *under* the catch in seizing the revolver, and press your thumb towards the palm of your hand in making the wrench.

With solid frame revolvers, like the new Colt and the Smith & Wesson, you operate the catch, and instead of twisting your wrist you push out the cylinder with your first and second fingers, at the same time pushing the extractor plunger with your little finger. This make of revolver, however, is more difficult to disarm suddenly than those I have named above.

With any hammer revolver you can make it harmless by slipping your thumb under the hammer, as Gastinne-Renette's assistants always hand you a loaded duelling pistol, or, if you are strong in the grip, by holding the cylinder and preventing its revolving after the first shot is fired.

I saw a very good suggestion in an article in an American paper— the writer's name I unfortunately forget—to the effect that it was an excellent thing, when expecting "trouble," to wear a big revolver ostentatiously and to have a smaller one in your hand, concealed under a cape, or otherwise; your adversary would think himself safe as long as he watched your big revolver and saw that you had not put your hand near it, whilst all the time you would be ready to "hold him up" or shoot with the other revolver, the existence of which he would not suspect.

If a burglar is in your house, do not carry a candle, as that makes you an easy target in case he should try to shoot at you. If you can get to the electric light switch unobserved, aim in his direction and then turn up the light so that you have the drop on him as the light appears and he will be at your mercy. The iron rails of banisters, especially if they are wide, ornamental ones, are a good protection. A door is of no use (except for concealment *before* the man has seen you), as a bullet with an ordinary charge will go through it.

Use a light charge (gallery ammunition by preference) for house

POSITION FOR SHOOTING AT AN ADVANCING OBJECT

protection, or you may shoot some of your family through a thin wall when "burglar-potting."

Out-of-doors, too, a lamp-post, or other narrow object, will spoil a man's aim by making him try to hit that part of you which shows on either side instead of his having your full width to aim at, even if it is too narrow or small fully to protect you.

It is better not to try to give him a small mark to aim at by standing sideways, as then, if he hits you, he will rake all through your vitals; whereas if you are facing him squarely he may put several bullets into you without fatal effect.. Holding your bent arm across your heart, and at the same time protecting your temples with the side of your revolver,—which duellists do directly they have fired,—may be of some use; but it is better to depend upon hitting your adversary before he hits you. If he shoots and misses you, drop at once, as if hit, and keep still, when he will probably pause and give you a chance to shoot.

If a man does not look desperate and capable of continuing shooting until killed it may be sufficient if you can break his shooting wrist: while if he should then try to shift his pistol from the disabled hand to the other, you can break the other also.

Should you be mounted and your adversary is on foot, jumping off and sheltering yourself behind your horse will protect you from a revolver-shot; also galloping hard at him and shouting may spoil his aim. If, on the contrary, he is cool, he may take an easy shot at you by dodging and shooting as you pass.

If a man is running away from, or coming at you, and has no firearm, you can make him helpless by shooting him in a leg; a long crossing shot in a bad light would make the leg shot rather doubtful, unless there be time to have several tries.

If a man absolutely has to be killed, it is better to shoot where the white shirt shows in evening dress. This is a bigger mark than the head, and he may, moreover, duck his head as you pull.

The stomach shot is a murderous one, and would not be justifiable except under very rare circumstances. A charging man at very close range would have the wind knocked out of him, and be stopped perhaps more effectually by this shot than any other.

If your opponent is a bad shot, you can take a long shot at him from a distance, say 120 yards, at which, if he has a cheap revolver, he cannot hit you except by a fluke, and it would not do much harm even if he did hit you.

In fact a bad shot armed with a revolver is less dangerous than a strong, determined man with a knife. It must be remembered that a knife can be thrown some distance, so it does not do to let a man with one in his hand, or even suspected of having one, come too close, especially in the dark.

A cartridge loaded with salt is a good man-stopper for burglars and has the advantage of not endangering life, but of course it is of no use against a determined man unless he is shot in the face. In that case salt might do even more damage to his eyes than a bullet, and a bullet would be a more merciful load.

The pamphlet on *Self-Defence*, says that to put the revolver beside the head of the bed, or under the pillow, is to court being disarmed during your sleep, and it recommends having it between the mattresses, handy to your reach, or in a padded bag hanging at the side of your bed, under the sheets, the object of the padding being to prevent the revolver from making a noise against the bed when you are drawing it.

This is all very well if you remember to take out the revolver each morning; if you forget, and the housemaid makes up the bed roughly, there may be trouble.

It also advises rolling under a bed or sofa as a precaution when exchanging shots.

Make sure that nobody can tamper with your revolver or cartridges. I knew of a case in which a muzzle-loading revolver was kept loaded in an unlocked box at the side of the bed. When there was a burglary in the house, this revolver was found to have been *soaked in water* and thus rendered useless!

COLT DERRINGER
.41 calibre, rim fire

137

CHAPTER 22

Pistol Shooting for Ladies

A revolver puts the weakest woman, who is a good shot, on an equality with the strongest man. It is especially suitable for ladies to defend themselves with, as they have, as a rule, steadier hands than men, and there are certain revolvers, just suited for ladies, which give no recoil and yet are serviceable weapons. "U. M. C." gallery ammunition in a .44 calibre Smith & Wesson Russian Model gives practically no recoil, and I have seen a lady do very good target shooting with it. With this revolver and load I have killed three rabid, or alleged rabid dogs, so it is a practical killing load. I use the same revolver and ammunition for shooting park bucks.

Every lady should, to my mind, know how to use a pistol. She may at any time be in China, or some other country where there are savage natives; and there is none of that danger of bruising the body which is so harmful to women using guns or rifles.

The Smith & Wesson hammerless safety revolvers of .38 and .32 calibre are especially suitable for self-defence for ladies, but I should not recommend a lady to use these or any other short, light, self-defence revolvers for target shooting, as the recoil is heavy and apt to hurt a lady's hand (particularly between the first finger and thumb) and tear the skin. This is inevitable in a revolver made as light and as portable as possible, and expected, nevertheless, to shoot a very heavy charge.

The best plan is to fire a few shots (the hand being protected with a thick driving glove, from which the forefinger has been cut off), or, better still, ask a good shot, who also knows your "sighting," to do so for you, just to get the sights filed right, and then keep this pistol for self-defence only, and do practising and competing with a more accurate and more pleasant shooting weapon.

The revolver or pistol to be used for practice and in competitions must depend upon your physique. If you are moderately strong, I think the .44 calibre Russian Model Smith & Wesson, with the Union Metallic Cart-ridge Co.'s gallery ammunition, is as good as any; or, if this is too heavy, the .38 or .32 calibre Colt and Smith & Wesson revolvers, with gallery ammunition, are very good and are specially intended for the use of ladies.

The Smith & Wesson .32 calibre in .44 calibre frame, which I like for fifty-yards target shooting, is rather heavy for a lady. Its size is an advantage for a man, as he can hold steadier with some little weight in his hand. Ladies who are of slight build may find it too heavy; but with gallery ammunition it has no recoil whatever, which is a great advantage for them.

Always have a barrel not shorter than five inches, and not longer than six inches, and save the weight, if you want a light weapon, in the general make-up of the revolver rather than in length of barrel, as you lose so much accuracy with a three-inch or four-inch barrel that it spoils any pleasure in shooting.

If you confine yourself to light ammunition, you can get a very light revolver which is safe with *that* charge, and has no recoil to speak of.

The Smith & Wesson, which has interchangeable barrels of .32 calibre for revolver, and .22 for single-shot pistol, is a very suitable weapon for a lady.

The lighter forms of single-shot Stevens pistols of .22 calibre and the Leeson .22 are exceptionally well adapted to the use of ladies who prefer a single-shot pistol. I have seen a very neat .22 calibre revolver of Belgian make with a six-inch barrel and cylinder very small in diameter, which makes it balance beautifully, but I do not know how it shoots or how the Colt .22 shoots.

In mentioning particular firms, both here and elsewhere in this book, I must not be misunderstood to mean that the weapons of any one maker are better than those of another. All first-class makers turn out good revolvers and pistols; and I merely mention those revolvers and pistols which I have used and am personally acquainted with, and which I find answer my requirements.

A lady can carry a revolver for self-defence hidden in many more ways than a man can, owing to her draperies affording more places for concealment. Cloaks, capes, etc., make good hiding-places for a revolver; inside a muff is about one of the best places; and a small revolver in the right hand, inside a muff, that hand hanging down by the side, is ready for instant use. As ladies often carry their muffs in this way, it does not arouse suspicion.

It is very important for ladies to protect their ears when shooting.

I do not consider an air gun a very suitable weapon for ladies' use; it has such a very bad, heavy dragging trigger pull that it does no good for rifle practising, it balances badly, and is generally heavier than a .22 short cartridge rifle can be made. Also, the lever for compressing the spring makes it balance badly, making it heavy forward, and the grip is big, in fact it is not the weapon I would recommend; its noiselessness, which is its only recommendation, is really more an imaginary than a real advantage, the short .22 (especially out-of-doors with smokeless powder) making hardly any report.

Also, compressing the spring is hard work for a lady; the butt has to be pressed against the leg, and the lever is apt to spring back and smash the fingers.

In criticising a former book of mine on shooting, a newspaper said it was fit only to teach extremely rich people shooting, as I advocated such expensive methods of practising. It instanced, as an example of this expense, my saying that one ought to get someone to compress the spring of the air gun between shots, as doing so oneself made the hands tired and shaky.

Now, with all respect to the paper in question, I think a lady can find some male friend who will undertake to work the lever and load the air gun for her without his charging anything; or she could even find a servant to do this who would not want a raise in wages in consequence.

If a tie has to be shot off in a few hours, it is best to try and get a rest, and, if possible, to sleep, during the interval. If this is impossible, reading an interesting book (if the type is not too small to tire the eyes), or playing some game, anything to take the thoughts off the approaching shoot-off, is good.

Finally I would add that when a lady sits on the ground to shoot off both knees, or lies down to shoot, or even if she sits on a chair or stands, out-of-doors, it is most important that she should be protected against dampness and chills, consequently she will do well to stand on a thick mat, and avoid linen underwear. The safest sort of garments are thick flannel knickerbockers.

CHAPTER 23

Shooting from a Bicycle

Fortunately in most countries there is seldom necessity to carry a loaded revolver on a bicycle. An empty one is sufficient to frighten away tramps, if they stop you on a dark, lonely road; or even a short bicycle pump when pointed at them may scare them off. One can, however, get some sport on a bicycle with a revolver.

I have described in the chapter on Self-defence one form of bicycle revolver; but for sport I should use a game-shooting one, as a bicycle revolver is not meant for anything but self-defence at short range. This latter would have to be carried in a holster strapped on the front fork, a method which is safer in case of a fall than when worn in a belt.

One can, with a little practice, shoot quite well off a bicycle, especially if, when actually aiming, the cyclist is "free-wheeling." The action of pedalling spoils one's aim.

A dog flying at your leg, when he comes up in his usual pleasant way from behind to bite you in the calf, would make a pretty shot; you could put up the leg he is going for and shoot down past your thigh, but might hear from his owner if he should happen to be in sight.

A cartridge loaded with coarse salt (as I have recommended for burglars) would stop a dog well, and teach him not to annoy cyclists; but then, in all probability, you would have not only the owner after you, but the Society for the Prevention of Cruelty to Animals as well. The Devilliers bullet is very good for this style of shooting practice and would be good to stop dogs at close quarters.

A bicycle gives one many good chances at deer, hares, rabbits, etc., in the early morning or evening, when going silently along by a river in a game country.

With a Gastinne-Renette pistol, shooting shot, or a .22 single-shot pistol, one could get lots of small game; but I must not go on, or this chapter will resolve itself into hints to poachers!

The weak point of the revolver as an arm for cyclists in war is the difficulty of shooting at pursuers. A horse can be left to pick his own way, but a cyclist who looks behind him is apt not only to lose his balance, but to run into something, and has also to slacken speed unless he merely blazes away behind him at random without either sitting up or looking back.

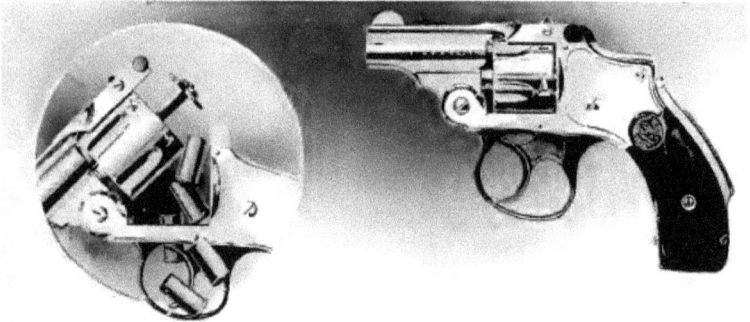

AUTOMATIC EXTRACTOR   SMITH & WESSON BICYCLE REVOLVER

CHAPTER 24

Revolvers for the Police

I have on several occasions attempted to get a prize accepted, to be competed for by the police, at Bisley, but each time unsuccessfully.

I then gave a statuette, modelled by myself as a revolver prize, open to the whole of the United States. The conditions were:

Any revolver; maximum length of barrel, including cylinder, ten inches. Any trigger-pull. Any sight, both sights to be on the barrel or forward of the grip of the pistol hand. Any fixed ammunition. Cleaning allowed only between scores of six shots. Distance, twenty yards. Position, standing, free from any artificial support, the revolver to be held in one hand only, with the arm free from the body and unsupported in any way. The rear sight not to be nearer to the eye than twelve inches.

Target.—Ready-measurement discs, one shot on each disc, and the measurement to be taken by mechanical Vernier scale, from the centre of disc to the centre of shot-hole.

Scores.—Aggregate of best three in five scores. Each score to consist of six consecutive rounds. The five scores to be fired consecutively.

Amateur Standing.—The standing of a contestant as amateur and professional to be determined in each individual case by *Forest and Stream* [this journal had charge of the competition]. Where not in conflict with the conditions herein, the rules of the Massachusetts Rifle Association for revolver competitions to hold. The decision of *Forest and Stream* to be final on all points.

Any winner of the trophy to hold it, subject to a challenge, for the term of two years, after which time it shall become his personal property. Upon receiving a challenge, the holder to agree with the challenger upon a place and date for their meeting not later than six weeks from the receipt of the challenge, of which meeting at least two weeks' notice shall be given through *Forest and Stream*, and the shooting at the said meeting to be under the same conditions as the original competition for the trophy. In case of a failure to agree upon a time and place of meeting, these to be fixed by *Forest and Stream*.

The trophy to be deposited in the custody of *Forest and Stream* at least one day prior to the challenge meet; and, if required, holders to give bonds to *Forest and Stream* for its safe return.

The holder not to be required to accept a challenge pending the determination of a challenge shoot already under date. In case of any dispute about the right of priority in shooting challenges, *Forest and Stream* to determine the order of shooting. All expenses of targets and gallery to be borne by *Forest and Stream*. Contestants to defray all other expenses.

This was a great success, and revolver-shots in most of the great cities of the United States competed for the trophy, which was held by Dr. Louis Bell, of the New York Pistol and Revolver Club, for the first time.

The trophy passed to two successful challengers, and finally became, in 1894, the property of Roundsman Petty, of the New York police force, who twice successfully defended his title.

The police of the United States were so pleased with this competition, that it is now the custom in some cities to have regular competitions for the members of the force; and many others besides Petty have become fine shots in consequence. Petty, however, was always a good shot.

People say: "Oh, if a policeman had a revolver he would be likely to shoot a man instead of arresting him." In my opinion, it would make a policeman less apt to hurt his man; and one would not hear so much of policemen being knocked down and kicked to death. If the policeman were known to be armed with a revolver, and had the "marksman's" badge on his uniform, it would have a salutary effect on roughs, who would think twice before attacking him; and he, in the confidence of his skill with the revolver, would act calmly, and shoot only as a last resource.

Only quite recently there was a report of a mad dog in a crowded street of New York. The policeman on the beat killed it at the first shot, and did not hit anyone in the crowd. Contrast this with the number of shots fired at the two anarchists in London lately, (1911).

If a London policeman were to start "loosing off" a revolver in a crowd, I fear the ambulance corps would be kept busy!

CHAPTER 25

Shooting in the Dark

There are occasions on which it is necessary to shoot at night, as for a night-watchman; or in the case of a wild animal's jumping into camp and carrying off someone; or in night attacks.

For this work an exceptionally large *dead white* front sight (either a fixed one or an adjustable one on a hinge or one kept for handiness in the stock of the revolver, that can be fitted on when necessary) is needful. This sort of sight, though, can be seen only if there is moonlight, or at least some glimmer of light.

In pitch-darkness, a large front sight with both itself and the rib of the barrel coated with luminous paint is useful, provided the revolver is, for several hours previous to its being used, exposed to strong sunlight. If the revolver be kept all day in a case or a holster, the paint will not shine at night. Also, in cleaning the revolver, the paint may be spoilt, and may require renewing. I would not advise painting any revolver you care about.

My patent electric rifle sight for night shooting is at present too cumbersome for application to a revolver; moreover, as I remark below, one ought to be able to use a revolver at short range by sense of direction, without looking along sights.

This is perhaps the most satisfactory way,—learning to shoot in the dark *by the sense of direction*, by pointing your revolver in the direction in which you conjecture the object to be, not by attempting to see your sights or to "draw a bead."

One can often see an animal on a very dark night by crouching down and getting it against the sky-line; and yet, on looking through the sights, you cannot discern anything.

One form of practice is to have a target made of tissue paper, with a candle behind it to illuminate it. The sights are consequently seen

Pocket Colt Double-Action Revolver

Police Colt Double-Action Revolver

in silhouette against it. This was the principle of the "Owl" series of prizes shot for in the early days of Wimbledon in the evenings. What I think better, so as to teach shooting by *sense of direction*, is to have several metal targets about a foot in diameter, hung by wires (these will give out a ringing sound when struck, and the rest of the butt should be of sand, or sods, or wood, so as to make a different sound). Have a small bell hung behind the middle of each target, pulled by a string, or an electric bell operated by strings held by an assistant standing behind you.

Now let him ring the bells at random, you firing by sense of direction towards where you hear each bell ring.

This practice can also be done in a shooting-gallery at night with all the lights turned down, and it is perhaps safer there than out-of-doors.

You can even have targets behind you, and swing round and "snap" at them; but this, and in fact all night shooting, is very dangerous unless you can be absolutely certain that the bullets will do no damage, however wildly they may fly, or unless you use Devilliers bullets.

A man with a good ear can do surprisingly accurate work in this style of shooting.

Such practice can be done in daylight by being blind-folded; and then your assistant can notice where your misses go, and help you to improve your shooting.

I will describe my patent electric sight, though it is too complicated for a revolver.

The object of my invention is to facilitate the sighting of firearms in the dusk or at night.

To this end I adapt to the weapon an electrical front sight and an electric battery with a minute incandescent lamp.

In the accompanying drawing I have shown my invention as applied to a rifle, by way of example.

Fig. 1 is a side view of the rifle complete, with my invention applied thereto.

Fig. 2 is a similar view, partly in section, showing the battery inside the stock.

Fig. 3 is a rear-end view of the rifle.

Figs. 4 and 5 are front views on an enlarged scale of a double- and single-barrelled rifle respectively, with an electric front sight affixed thereto.

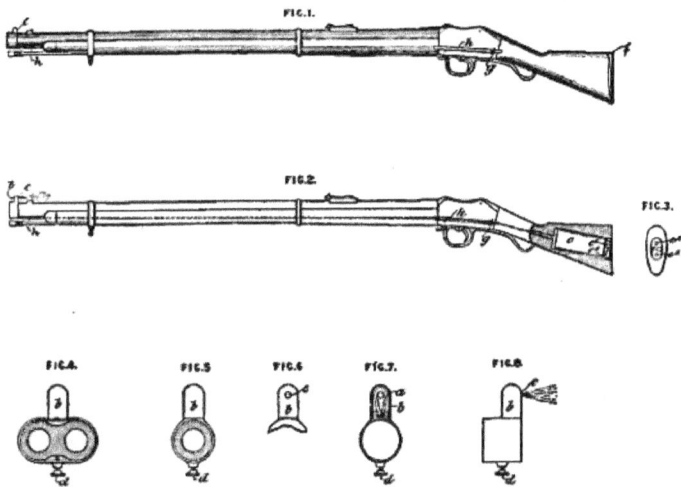

Fig. 6 represents the sight as seen by the shooter.

Fig. 8 is a side view of the lamp case.

The incandescent lamp a (made as small as practicable) is enclosed in a metal case b in which is a small hole c facing the shooter, so that a bright spot of light appears just above or on a line with the ordinary fixed sight of the weapon when the current from the generator or battery is passing. The lower part of the case b is of a form to fit round the barrel and is provided with a small clamping screw d by which it can be secured in the proper position.

The aperture c is protected by a piece of glass, and a reflector is arranged within the case b opposite, thus making a miniature electrical bull's-eye or dark lantern of the lamp. The lamp is mounted on a spring or springs after the manner commonly practised with respect to incandescent lamps, and is packed round with cotton-wool, horsehair, or other elastic substance to prevent breakage by the concussion of the rifle on discharge.

The switch g is fixed at a point suitable for operation by the shooter in the act of aiming. It may act automatically when the butt is presented to the shoulder or when the grip is squeezed, or it may be connected with the hammer or striker so that when the rifle is at full-cock the front sight glows, and when the trigger is pressed the light goes out.

The battery is only of such power as to make the lamp glow

sufficiently to enable the shooter to see it plainly; as it would otherwise, if too bright, prevent his seeing the object aimed at.

I think I have now given directions how to handle the pistol under most of the circumstances and occasions in which one would have use for it; and I have also, I hope, shown that it can be employed as a more workmanlike and a neater tool than a rifle or a scatter-gun in cases in which the uninitiated would not think of using it.

The revolver is popularly looked upon as an "extinguisher," and I may now, having finished writing for the present, extinguish my candle with one.

www.ingramcontent.com/pod-product-compliance
Lightning Source LLC
Chambersburg PA
CBHW021005090426
42738CB00007B/659